The
Butterfly
Gardener

MIRIAM ROTHSCHILD & CLIVE FARRELL

Illustrated by Elisabeth Luard

MICHAEL JOSEPH / RAINBIRD

To the memory of Rory McEwen
who loved butterflies & flowers

First published in Great Britain 1983 by
Michael Joseph Ltd,
44 Bedford Square, London WC1 and
The Rainbird Publishing Group Ltd,
40 Park Street, London W1Y 4DE
who designed and produced the book

ISBN: 0 7181 2258 5

Typeset by Inforum Ltd, Portsmouth
Illustrations originated by
Adroit Photo Ltd, Birmingham
Printed and bound by
Mackays of Chatham Ltd, Chatham, Kent

Frontispiece, red admirals and a hornet sharing ripe plums

Contents

Acknowledgments

Miriam Rothschild is immensely grateful to Kazuo Unno for the use of four of his photographs (facing p. 16; on the right, between pp. 16 and 17; facing p. 17), which are among the most beautiful butterfly pictures ever taken, and to Paul Whalley for much helpful criticism, and the chart on p. 118.

Clive Farrell wishes to thank all those who have helped with the production of this book, and the creation of the London Butterfly House itself.

First, his thanks to his wife Rajna for her great patience with an obsessive butterfly maniac, and her support throughout.

Next, he would like to acknowledge the help, advice, information and gifts of living material received from his co-author Miriam Rothschild; also Claude Rivers, Cyril Clarke, Roy Stockley, Brian O.C. Gardiner and Derek Arthurs, John Stone, Bob Bowle and staff at the University of London Botanical Supply Unit, Clive Urich, Keith Croxford, David Goh, Robert Goodden, Bill and Helen Luker, Eddie Tobler, Bert Barnett and staff at Norwood Hall Horicultural School, Brian Wurzell, Ian Wallace of Entomological Livestock Supplies, James Gardner, Jim Hendriksen and his two sons Andre and Anton, Gweneth Johnston and Brian Smith.

He is particularly indebted to his secretary, Stella Smith, who helped him throughout, deciphering his awful handwriting which included many strange Latin names.

Both authors are grateful for the care and attention lavished on the production of this volume by Karen Goldie-Morrison and Peter Coxhead of Rainbird.

The publisher would like to thank: Tony Evans for the use of his photograph of chalk grassland (between pp. 16 and 17); Carl Wallace for his photographs (which appear on the spread between pp. 80 and 81, and facing p. 81); also Susan Conder for designing and drawing the plan of the butterfly garden (on pp. 54 and 55).

The Outdoor Butterfly Gardener

MIRIAM ROTHSCHILD

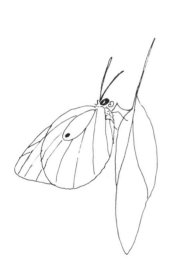

Introduction

I have assumed, in writing this book, that the reader's garden has been laid out years ago and the trees planted, and that he or she is well-versed in the basic principles of everyday gardening. So that I have not described how to plant an ash tree, or a beech hedge, or prune a rose, take a cutting, pull up dock, dig in manure or clean the mowing machine. Only a little gardening information is supplied about a few common garden plants, which are seen to be especially attractive or important to butterflies. On the other hand I have paid more attention to the cultivation of wild flowers, for this is a new venture about which very little is known. In fact anyone who attempts to do so can record his own observations and be sure that some of them at least will be 'new' and all will be interesting to other wild-flower gardeners. Nor have I treated the reader to any conventional entomology but I have supplied a few notes in the appendix. I regard butterflies as a wonderful bonus in the garden and have suggested ways by which we can entice them in and persuade them to stay for as long as possible and in this fashion help conserve them. I have not dwelt upon their structure, physiology or evolution.

I hope that these few notes will show that it is rewarding and inexpensive to grow wild flowers. There is a very curious aspect to this relatively new hobby. Once you have turned your attention to buttercups and daisies or scarlet pimpernels you begin to find the familiar well-loved garden flowers beautiful but dull. It's something I find hard to explain, but true: I think butterflies feel the same way.

Those of us who own small gardens in London or the suburbs cannot expect to attract as many insects as the lucky ones who live in the country. But it is as well to reflect that a butterfly and moth survey in the garden at Buckingham Palace – in the heart of London – during 1960–4 revealed the presence of 344 species of Lepidoptera, of which two had not previously been reported from the U.K.! Among the butterflies caught were two of the nymphalids – red admiral, small tortoiseshell – the holly blue and two whites, and among the moths privet hawk, cinnabar and garden tiger. So London gardeners can be reasonably optimistic.

As for the Royal Parks and open spaces like St James's Park, here the opportunities for wild flowers and butterflies are enormous. The time has come when bedding-out is too costly and a flowering grass mixture will take the place of formal arrangements. Very soon school children will learn about their native wild flora and the attendant butterflies in the flower walk in Kensington Gardens.

Perhaps the greatest future for wild-flower cultivation and the conservation of our butterflies lies in introducing the appropriate floral mixtures into paddocks surrounding country houses and along motorways and bypasses. Success will depend on modifying farm machinery to harvest and sow wild-flower seed, in conjunction with horticultural propagation. His Royal Highness the Prince of Wales is a pioneer in this experimental field, for in the paddocks at Highgrove he has sown the first big sample of combine-harvested wild-flower seed together with a hand-picked mixture of carefully selected native species grown in rows in the kitchen garden.

Gardening with Butterflies

I garden purely for pleasure. I love plants and flowers and green leaves and I am incurably romantic – hankering after small stars spangling the grass. Butterflies add another dimension to the garden for they are like dream flowers – childhood dreams – which have broken loose from their stalks and escaped into the sunshine. Air and angels. This is the way I look upon their presence – not as a professional entomologist, any more than I look upon roses as a botanist might – complaining that they are an impossibly 'difficult group'.

I divide my garden into three rather distinct sections. Firstly, a conventional stone-walled kitchen garden with some half-derelict glasshouses in the middle. A variety of fruit trees – morello cherries, apricots, peaches, pears, greengages and so forth are grown along the inside of the wall. Plants are cultivated in rows, in trays or in pots; the soil is a mixture of rich loams, some of it originally brought from the Bournemouth area – heaven knows why! – by goods train, around the turn of the century. After eighty years in constant cultivation with the use of an absolute minimum of sprays and insecticides, I fancy it harbours more than an average share of undesirable organisms. But that may be just an excuse when things go wrong – the 1980 epidemic of crown rot and red spider, for instance.

The second well-defined area is the house itself and the courtyard round which it is built. Here I have planted a wide variety of creepers and wall-trained shrubs for all seasons, ranging from Japanese quince and wisteria to *Rosa banksii*, bittersweet, bryonies and varieties of clematis including traveller's-joy or old man's beard. There is a fine profusion of garden flowers and wild species where stone and soil meet round the foundations, in a sort of grassy border. A visitor arriving for the first time in this courtyard looked round at the untamed creepers and broom and the mauve and blue haze of candytuft and flax growing out of the gravel and, before ringing the bell, remarked uneasily: 'I don't believe anyone can LIVE here . . .'

Nymphalid and white butterflies from the flower beds are lured by tall shrubs to an upper-storey window

11

Finally, the third area consists of an acre of flowering hayfield, divided from the house itself and its surrounding belt of flowers by a strip of closely cut lawn, a long bank of uncut grass and well-spaced-out wild cherry trees – by far and away my favourite tree – lilac bushes, a young ash or two, with wild honeysuckle climbing up their branches and a few crab apples, also growing in the long grass. The edges of a gravel path provide an additional mini-habitat.

Modern agricultural methods are unfortunately lethal both to wild flowers and butterflies. Cowslips and buttercups, and blue and copper wings have been cultivated, drained and bulldozed out of our fields. The smell of new-mown hay has been replaced by diesel fumes and clouds of dust, while instead of haycocks, giant circular machine-made bales stand incongruously in the fields like the droppings of some mechanical monster. But with time and trouble and experimentation one can get wild flowers to grow in profusion in the grass or mixed in with the good old cultivated varieties. Thus we can entice a few butterflies back into our daily lives, and hope they will dawdle and dally round the *Buddleia*. Wordsworth, in one of his most dreadful poems, had the same thought:

> *Stay near me – do not take thy flight,*
> *A little longer stay in sight.*
> *Much converse do I find in thee*
> *Historian of my infancy.*

But you can really abandon any romantic idea of creating a *home* for these angelic creatures – the best you can do is to provide them with a good pub. And like all popular wayside inns it must have a plentiful supply of standard drinks always on tap.

Why do butterflies like some flowers more than others? Why is the taste and aroma of *Buddleia* nectar so infinitely more to their liking than the perfume and flavour of roses? We do not know. The fact is we know very little indeed about butterflies, but it is clear they prefer heavy perfume to delicate scents, and they must have the carbohydrates which they find in nectar – for flight demands a lot of energy. This secretion is, broadly speaking, an aqueous solution of sugar of which there are basically three types: one which contains sucrose (cane sugar), one fructose (fruit sugar, which is the sweetest of the common sugars), and glucose (corn or grape sugar). Sometimes all three sugars occur in the nectar of one species. The plants advertise the presence of this vital food source by a delicious variety of scent and colour. The butterflies themselves exhale a delightful flowery fragrance. On a sunny day this mixture is like an umbrella of perfume spread across the garden, exciting the butterfiles sexually, while the flowers are offering themselves freely in the interest of procreation. It is worth noting that where taste and smell are concerned, butterflies are superior to ourselves. They not only have chemical receptors on their tongues and antennae, but also on their feet. They can discriminate between the substance in Indian hemp which gives us a 'high' and the cannabidiol which does not, whereas to our relatively feeble nose these two are indistinguishable.

Abraham Cowley in 'The Wish' says: 'May I a small house and a large garden have', and this I believe is the right approach – even with a dearth of hands which leads inescapably to a wilderness, I doubt a garden can ever be too large. Certainly not from the butterfly's viewpoint. But so many of us are forced to be satisfied with a small patch of ground that it is an agreeable thought that butterflies can be attracted to tiny gardens as well as large ones. A *Buddleia* planted against your house, a patch of red valerian growing out of a wall, or a lavender bush constitutes a true butterfly lure. Like Alfred Tennyson, I favour 'a careless order'd garden', though growing wild flowers is no easier than cultivating the conventional, well-tried horticultural varieties. In some ways it is more difficult because not much is known about them. I doubt if you can easily find a book which tells you how to grow the lesser celandine or selfheal in a garden – or how to keep order in a little wilderness. Nor for that matter are wild flowers essential as butterfly lures, but they are a great help. Moreover it is one way of not only preserving the wild species from extinction – for who can doubt that cowslips will one day be as rare as the lady's-slipper orchid, thanks to our sprays and combines and ditching equipment – but also providing special nectar sources for butterflies.

A new type of municipal horticulture is just round the corner – when the parks in new towns, and the road verges and roundabouts will be sown with a flowering-meadow mixture instead of a dreary mono-crop of coarse grass. The rise in the price of fuel has done us one good turn – it has reduced the needless cutting of road verges and in many areas the wild flowers are already enhancing our dreary motorways. This roadside flora turns the verges into *butterfly highways* – a link between woods and Nature Reserves which have rapidly become like a series of oases in a desert of sprayed and smoking cornfields. Road cuttings with steep banks are ideal sunny spots for both wild flowers and butterflies. If you have a bank in your garden, cherish it.

About 200 years ago Addison in the *Spectator* remarked that he valued his garden 'for being fuller of blackbirds than of cherries'. I agree with him, although there are times when you sigh and wish it were otherwise. Last summer I watched with mixed feelings a charm of goldfinches descend on a row of goat's-beard and pick them to pieces and rob the seed before the 'clocks' developed. I was saving them all carefully for sowing. But no one in their senses would exchange goldfinches for a row of goat's-beard, however fascinating their huge 'clocks' may be. I encourage all the birds, although bull-finches which demolish cherry and apple blossom – presumably looking for insects or even nectar? – are beautiful but pestilential and destructive creatures. And I have a passion for robins singing in the rain. I believe their songs to be outbursts of beautiful rage . . . I willingly sacrifice the odd butterfly for their sake. In a small garden you are much more conscious of insect pests, and snails, and field voles, than you are in a large one. You know each plant individually and it gets under your skin if you see your roses covered in greenfly, or the tender leaves chewed up by remorseless slugs, or half-opened cherry blossom littering the path, or foliage scalloped by leaf-cutting bees. But if you really want butterflies in the garden you have to reduce sprays to an absolute minimum and abstain from slug pellets. In my own garden, in the open, I have purchased no insecticides or weed killers or seed dressings for the last ten years, but I have sprayed diligently against fungi and green fly, in the latter case with a simple detergent, Lux, and I bring in every ladybird I can find – especially in the larval stage – and put them on the roses, hoping they will help to check the greenfly. Ladybirds, however, like butterflies, are apt to move on . . . Undoubtedly the birds destroy a lot of insects, both good and bad, and in the process take their toll of flower buds and seeds. The butterflies in their turn pollinate many of my flowers, though their young stages chew up the cabbages and nasturtium (*Tropaeolum*) leaves. But by and large I give nature a free hand, and I am rewarded by the fact that I have a pair of nightingales singing close to the house and at the moment of writing thirteen species of butterflies on the wing and over 100 species of wild flowers and grasses in the garden.

Spring in the Butterfly Garden

The brimstone butterfly is the herald of spring – even though hazel catkins in the hedge may actually beat them to it, and pollen begins to blow round the impossibly tiny red plume of their female stigmas in February and March. The brimstone is an extraordinary insect, for it seems to have a different texture from any other butterfly and might be cut out of yellow felt with firm thick edges. Its flight is slow and felt-like too – one is not surprised to learn it is our longest lived species. Because of its association with pale March sunshine and the sheer surprise of its appearance, it remains fixed in one's mind as the only true spring butterfly. Why don't the insect-starved birds which have over-wintered here demolish the slow flying, conspicuous brimstone? They have a long memory and may confuse it with the large whites of last autumn, which are severely left alone by most birds on account of their revolting taste. There has been a lot of speculation about this, but no one really knows.

A hedge is a very important part of the butterfly garden for butter-flies need shelter. It should be planted – in the open or along a fence or wall – with willows and sallows for the sake of their early catkins. The butterflies which awake from winter hibernation like small tor-toiseshells, brimstones, commas and peacocks have nothing better than sallow catkins for their important first feed of nectar, although I have planted some coltsfoot for them along the path – since the flowers open in March. Buckthorn or alder buckthorn must also be part of the hedge, for the brimstone lays on these plants and its caterpillars feed on the leaves, also it is one of the few droppers-in that might then become a resident. Blackthorn, hawthorn and privet are other desirable nectar plants for your hedge, but even more important are brambles (or blackberry) and raspberries which, in flower, are two of the greatest of butterfly lures. The spindle, because it is the winter host of black bean aphids, should not, in theory, be planted. But I find two things about it irresistible: firstly the fascinating contrast between its shocking-pink fruits which split open to reveal their orange seeds; secondly the fact that the beautiful black and white magpie moth feeds on its leaves – despite the heart poison in their sap. When I was a child this moth used to thrive in surburban gardens, but the motor car and its fumes, or perhaps the tarmac dust, appear to have reduced its numbers drastically. Another plant for the butterfly hedge is the wayfaring-tree which smells a bit like carnations, and, though nectarless, attracts clearwing moths – wasp-like creatures with transparent wings which escape their enemies by this form of mimicry. Do they eat pollen from the flowers like the numerous bee visitors? Or is it merely a food plant for their larvae? The red and black berries of the wayfaring-tree in the autumn are a bonus. Nor must you forget holly for the holly blue.

Blackthorn is a great favourite with Lepidoptera, while hawthorn is chiefly attractive to a wide variety of flies which pollinate them, although Hugh Newman (senior) declared that butterflies are very keen on these flowers too – but in any case who can possibly resist May frothing along the sides of a hedge for these few brief blue and golden days?

> *Theirs was the bitterness we know*
> *Because the clouds of Hawthorn keep*
> *So short a state and kisses go to tombs*
> *unfathomably deep . . .*

Grass gardeners can really enjoy the spring – it is the least arduous season from our point of view, and if bees rather than butterflies love the tulips and the daffodils, it does not seem to matter at all in March and April.

Immediately round the house, or climbing on the house, I have mixed up wild and cultivated flowers and can indulge in various weaknesses – some passing manias, others more durable – like my present fancy for mauve and blue flowers blooming together in close proximity: purple crocus and scillas, bluebells and aubrieta, or candytuft and flax, or chionodoxa and dame's-violet. The latter is a great favourite with the orange tip butterfly – only the male has orange tips to its wings, the female is white – both as a nectar source and food for its caterpillars. It is so much easier to grow than lady's smock (although, irritatingly enough, a biennial not a perennial). The latter, which is the orange tip's first choice, likes damp feet – water meadows – as well as a humid atmosphere. It grows in great sheets in

Opposite, a peacock butterfly's first spring morning. Overleaf, flowers and grasses suitable for a chalky or limestone soil include lady's bedstraw, selfheal, wild thyme, squinancy wort and Timothy-grass

16

Normandy, for instance, and if you have a soggy piece of lawn in your own garden it might do very well indeed. It is a strange fact that you can mow a lawn in the spring year after year, but if you stop, the lady's smock reappear as if they had never been prevented from flowering or seeding for one, let alone a score, of seasons. This raises an interesting question: has this power of persisting underground developed as a defence against defoliation by lepidopterous larvae? We sometimes forget the tangle of roots below the soil surface. One plant of barley, for instance, has over eleven miles of root. A great battle must be taking place silently in the dark.

The orange tip roosts on the flower head of lady's smock, well concealed by its camouflaged underside, but after the females have fallen asleep (about 4.45 p.m.) randy males quarter the area searching for possible mates. Once spotted, the females are unceremoniously knocked out of bed and violated; if already mated they defend themselves vigorously, but no virgin is allowed to retire for the night unfertilized. Butterflies are ephemeral but brutal creatures – they fight fiercely over nectar sources and rape is commonplace. It is quite usual for a male to be sexually assaulted by another male if they feel in that mood. If our ears were as good as the ears of moths we could hear their wings clashing overhead.

In the grass round the courtyard and immediately in front of the house I have transplanted thousands of cowslip seedlings grown from seed in the kitchen garden. These were put directly into the sward along with a few thousand wild bluebells, also originally grown from seed, with the addition of miniature daffodils, tulips, fritillaries, plenty of dandelions and ramsons or wild garlic. They form an attractive mixture of wild and cultivated flowers and bloom profusely in the short grass – like an old fashioned Flemish tapestry.

At this stage the hayfield is more natural – the plants are not so crowded – and it is quite simply a cowslip meadow, with the odd lady's smock and two plants of the pasqueflower, which I fancy were introduced by a friend when my back was turned. I can't believe their seeds were blown here from the Hills and the Holes National Nature Reserve at Barnack about 18 miles distant. But they hold their own. From the butterfly's point of view the hayfield is far too windy, for it is exposed to the full force of the western gales blowing up from the Nene Valley. It would have been a very simple matter to plant a belt of protective trees and bushes along this edge and turn it into a sunny, sheltered dell instead of an open wind-swept meadow, but

Opposite, a white butterfly in the garden. Previous page, a painted lady, the great traveller, feeding from dandelions

Orange tip going to roost
on a lady's smock

the butterflies were quite ruthlessly sacrificed to the view!

The Duke of Burgundy fritillary is the butterfly which lays its eggs on cowslips in May, but with the reduction of its foodplant it has virtually vanished from Northamptonshire. In any case it is not likely to be attracted into your garden unless you have the luck to border a stretch of woodland. The same is true for the first brood of the sun-flecked speckled wood which, however, feeds as a caterpillar on grasses and has become commoner in recent years. In fact it has established a small breeding colony in at least one shady garden.

This season – with the pearl-bordered fritillary in mind – I want to plant seedling common dog- and sweet violets on the banks (this butterfly also feeds on pansies), although the grass may prove too strong for them. In the kitchen garden, without competition (i.e. in a weed-free bed) individual plants grow to an astonishing size, sometimes 18 inches across and covered with flowers. These blooms rarely set seed, but in late summer the plants produce many so-called cleistogomous buds on the lowest stems near the ground. These buds, which never open properly, are self-fertilized and produce plenty of fertile seeds. You may have to turn back the leaves to find them.

In April and May there are only relatively few butterflies on the wing, and one depends almost entirely on early bees or bee-like flies as pollinators. You will see the odd small tortoiseshell and peacock whisk past, settling briefly on the willow catkins, but there is no dallying so familiar in July and August. These are the spring broods which will have reproduction on their minds, for they must mate, find their foodplant, lay their eggs promptly and get the second broods under way. No fooling around . . . Butterflies, remarked Shakespeare, 'show not their mealy wings but to the summer'. But the very early comma will pause among the cherry blossom.

You may be lucky and the odd small copper will be drawn to the early flowers. It has three broods. I hesitate, but I still think this smart, metallic little spark of a butterfly is my favourite. It is amazingly pugnacious – chasing away any species which dare to enter its territory, which it marks like a dog – scratching excretions onto the surface of leaves. I once saw it sucking up so-called cuckoo spit – the froth surrounding frog hoppers – and becoming drunk in the process. What defensive, soporific, chemical, I wonder, does cuckoo spit contain? Another spring butterfly, the holly blue, which feeds as a caterpillar on ivy blossom and holly flowers, is enticed by a good tall specimen of this tree. It is a very pretty little thing, floating away erratically like a scrap of pale powder-blue paper in a gusty wind. But holly in hedges does not always produce flowers, so it is just as well to have a small tree somewhere in the sun; and ivy along your wall or concealing a shed – for it is the summer brood of this butterfly which lays its eggs on the buds of ivy, and the specimens you see haunting the holly in spring have fed on its flowers.

But the spring belongs to the white butterflies and the brimstone. The whites are so catholic in their tastes that you can satisfy them with a large array of spring flowers – primroses, polyanthus, dandelions . . . and of course all their larval foodplants (the cabbage family) like wallflowers, aubrieta and wild cabbage or rape. (This makes a beautiful, graceful cut flower too, especially in a tall glass vase.) The whites are great chemists and unerringly select plants for egg-laying which contain mustard oils, and these include mignonette and nasturtium (*Tropaeoleum*). These butterflies can assess the number of eggs laid on a plant. If they reckon there are enough to support one brood of caterpillars they move onto the next. They 'count' the number of eggs by using their eyes, antennae, the soles of their feet and a sensory organ on the tip of the abdomen. Now, whites may well become temporary residents and mar your cabbages. O.K. – use a fine fishnet to protect just those you need for your own table, leave the rest, and later on enjoy the newly emerged butterflies on the lavender.

Sometimes there seems to be a pause between spring and summer in the garden and this is bridged by a mist of Queen Anne's lace (a far nicer name than cow parsley) which has seeded along the grass banks, and through which shafts of early June sunrise filter to rouse the sleeping whites.

High Summer in the Butterfly Garden

In England, July and August are the months in which our most spectacular butterflies are on the wing.

The cultivated flowers which provide their favourite nectars are red valerian, *Buddleia*, *Sedum spectabile*, Michaelmas daisy, bramble, honeysuckle, lavender and a giant ragwort from China, *Ligularia dentata (Senecio clivorum)*. Flowers and insects have travelled down the ages together, bound up in a kaleidoscopic rainbow relationship of mutual benefit and mutual exploitation. In the garden pub the butterflies – in exchange for the nectar produced to attract them – effect pollination by fortuitously carrying the grains on their furry bodies from one flower to another. Since the more numerous they are, the more flowers will be fertilized, plants can afford to feed caterpillars on their own leaves. It is curious, however, that butterflies in England often lay eggs on the plants from which they do not gather nectar. Thus, for instance, fritillaries often feed as caterpillars on the leaves of violets, but these flowers are over by the time the adult is on the wing, nor do the larvae of our common butterflies feed on the leaves of *Buddleia*, which is so attractive as a nectar source to the adults. Similarly, small tortoiseshells, peacocks and red admirals which, as caterpillars, consume stinging nettles, do not obtain nectar from them – for these plants, like their relative, the elm tree, are wind pollinated and do not require the service of butterflies. The larva of the large tortoiseshell feeds on elms, but it is a woodland species, not to be expected in the garden.

Buddleia davidii (the genus named after the 17th-century botanist Adam Buddle) has a fruity smell and is certainly the standard liquor in any butterfly pub in Europe and North America. However, a really cold winter can cut it back drastically, or even kill the plant.

Personally I like placing *B. davidii* against the wall of my house – in this position it is adequately protected against even the severest weather. Also, if it is planted in an alcove formed by the meeting of two walls so that the lower part is shaded, or partially shaded, it will grow like a creeper, reaching for the light until it attains a height of between 15 and 20 feet. It then produces a cascade of flowers, a whiff of fruity honey, and a flight of butterflies round your bedroom window. Especially white ones; they seem to enjoy the height. Although the relatively hardy *B. davidii*, which flowers so freely late in July, is the butterfly's great favourite, you can extend the season from May to late September by selecting other species and their varieties. Hillier's catalogue of shrubs and trees gives a choice of fifty. Also you can induce the lateral branches to flower at the end of the season by cutting off faded terminal blooms. At the moment of writing (26 July, mid-morning), the following butterflies are on my *Buddleia*: small tortoiseshells and peacocks, one red admiral, one brimstone, one comma, several whites (three species), a meadow brown, several gatekeepers and a wall butterfly. Missing for the moment is the painted lady which is quite a common migrant visitor – one of the success stories of the butterfly world, for it is found from England to India, from below sea level to 18,000 feet in the Himalayas.

Butterflies and moths cannot chew; they have tubular mouth-parts adapted for sucking only, although a few thirsty moths in the tropics have graduated from drinking the tears of buffaloes to piercing their blood vessels and imbibing blood. They are also specialists in feeding from tubular flowers. The flowering heads of red valerian are a mass of tiny slender tubes. This comes into bloom before the *Buddleia* and in my garden at any rate grows like a weed – in stone walls, along gravel paths, in the paving stones, anywhere and everywhere, both the pink and white varieties. It is a great favourite with the elephant hawk-moth and the migrant hummingbird hawk-moth which crosses the Channel in mid-summer or later, and lays its eggs on lady's bedstraw. The former can be seen at dusk – its rosy underside merging in with the pink of the flowers. The hummingbird hawk-moth, on the contrary, at mid-day swerves like a miniature jet from valerian to valerian, although I once came across it in a mossy cave on a Greek island, tongue extended, wings whirring, working its way across the rock surface in the dim light – taking something which caught its fancy trickling down between the mosses. It is said only to drink very fluid substances. Many butterflies get round this problem by spitting into the flower tubes they suck, and so rendering the nectar less sticky and easier to draw up through their tubular tongues. To attract the large and rarer hawk-moths (which are also migrants) like the convolvulus hawk, it is advisable to add tobacco plants to your garden. They are wonderfully hardy annuals which seed themselves freely – the white varieties are favourites – and they expand their star-like corollas at dusk and, at the same time, pour out a heady perfume which I believe attracts these giant moths, although some entomologists think they find these flowers by their whiteness shining in the dim light. (The silver-Y moth, for instance, is said to locate its first meal of nectar by the scent of the flowers, but thereafter recognizes them by sight.) The tube of the tobacco plant flower is the right length for these distinguished droppers-in, for this hawk-moth's tongue is 65–80 mm long – a good match. It is also partial to scarlet geraniums (pelargoniums) – a strange contrast. It may arrive in your garden from Europe, Africa or even the Pacific, for it is a dedicated traveller. I once diverted a stream of these migrating jets into a moth-trap which I had set up on the seashore in Israel. When I picked one up it squeaked like a mouse. This noise is probably produced by blowing through its proboscis. A close relative, the privet hawk, has been caught in the garden of Buckingham Palace.

I push wild honeysuckle, as I have indicated, up every tree in my garden. I hope to attract white admirals which – who knows? – might lay on this plant after feeding on the *Buddleia*. In 1940 they were quite frequent visitors. Honeysuckle is another flower at its best, scent-wise, at dusk, as the moon rises, and the nightingales 'let their silver siftings fall'. The long-tongued noctuid moths, such as the plusias (which also fly by day), the gold spangle, burnished brass and silver-Y – also a great traveller – are irresistibly drawn to it. These moths are fine pollinators, although abroad some of them reach plague proportions and their caterpillars can eat you out of field and garden. They feed on almost any low-growing plant. The larvae of the gold spangle feeds on delphiniums and monks-hood – a good reason for growing these against the wall of the house among the tobacco plants. They also make a good background for a herbaceous border. I believe wild flowers should be used sparingly or not at all in some herbaceous borders. They do not like a rich, well-fertilized soil. The border can be packed with a variety of horticultural flowers. It is merely a question of the gardener's taste. For, as I have said before, butterflies enjoy a wide choice.

Bramble figures in my list of essentials for the butterfly pub. The cultivated variety has a larger bloom and flowers more freely than the wild type, and it is an exceedingly beautiful plant, cascading blossom over the fence, or lighting up a hedge, or growing as an isolated bush on either side of a door. Brambles have an especially copious flow of nectar which contains all three types of sugar, and in nature one can observe the same butterfly return again and again to the specific flowers on a bush.

The *Sedum spectabile* is almost an autumn flower, for it does not really open until September and blooms doggedly until mid-October. It is flat topped with a dirty pink inflorescence, which exerts a magical attraction for the small tortoiseshell (and certain species of bumble bees) and in good years it is so thickly covered with these butterflies that the flower heads are virtually hidden from view. Another great draw, but this time for red admirals, is the rather coarse overlarge *Ligularia clivorum*. It reveals the subtle differences in taste between related species, for the two butterflies both feed avidly side by side on *Buddleia* but are sorted into two quite distinct groups by *Sedum* and *Ligularia*. Frankly, I think the latter with its immense, almost rhubarb-like leaves, is ugly, but it can be planted against a wall or hide a shed, and there is nothing the red admirals love so much.

Lavenders – of several shades of pale mauve and dark purple – are best grown as a low hedge. There are various useful late flowering varieties. White and yellow butterflies swarm onto it and provide one of the most beautiful and evocative sights in the summer garden.

Apart from these standard drinks, the butterfly publican has a wide choice of attractive plants, since his clients love variety. All the Lepidoptera are partial to the daisy family (with heads of closely packed short tubular florets) from ragwort and Michaelmas daisy to golden rod and the wonderfully hardy indestructible globe thistles and dahlia – there are about 13,000 species in this family. They also fancy marjoram, catmint, sweet william and *Verbena*. The flowers of various cabbages – broccoli, cauliflower, rape and so forth – are attractive to the whites despite the fact that they are larval foodplants. If the lower leaves of these plants are removed, the flowers make a beautiful early yellow addition to the garden and, as I pointed out before, are marvellous as graceful cut blooms in the home. Cherry-pie or heliotrope is a great favourite with a wide variety of species – from whites to the comma. Vanilla is one of the most persistent and evocative scents, and heliotrope is loaded with it. More flowers and

Butterfly favourites. 1 *Sedum spectabile*; 2 *Lonicera periclymenum*; 3 *Buddleia*; 4 Michaelmas daisy; 5 *Verbena bonariensis*; 6 ivy; 7 bramble

more butterflies smell of vanilla than any other perfume, and it certainly possesses a subtly stimulating quality. The advertisements for chocolate – which is usually flavoured with vanilla – suggest that men and women, like butterflies, subconsciously find this scent sexually exciting.

Although some of these insects are conservative in their habits and appear to be hooked on one sort of flower or perhaps one particular colour, like purple or blue, I have not found this to be the usual state of affairs. Butterflies with their catholic tastes will often visit as many as twenty different flowers one after another if they are available – feeding on some or maybe only investigating them. According to various observers the large white prefers yellow-blue flowers when it is young, red-blue when it is older. While I have been writing these paragraphs, I have seen a large white visit selfheal, ragwort, red valerian, *Buddleia*, knapweed and dandelion – a mixture of colours. But on the whole I think they prefer yellow as nectar flowers.

In one way butterflies and moths are a disappointment, for they don't like roses and ignore them studiously. This is extremely odd in view of their inordinate fondness for bramble blossom, since both belong to the same family of plants. Poets still stick stubbornly to the notion that 'with the rose the butterfly's deeply in love'. But this is poetic licence – for they are basically beetle flowers, and these insects besides acting as pollinators often chew up and eat the petals and can be horribly destructive. This does not prevent my growing roses in my butterfly garden. I do not think we can often boast of improving upon nature, but there are two achievements of the human race I put rather high – one is floodlighting of tall trees and the other is the production of the dark crimson rose, 'Étoile de Hollande'. Some garden productions, for instance fleshy begonias the size of soup plates, or delphiniums like ultramarine telegraph poles, are vulgar in all conscience, but the Étoile is a flower which, as an achievement, puts the Apollo moon rocket in the shade. As for the wild dog rose – it is the most beautiful bush in the world. It has that air of insouciant disorder which only comes to a woman supremely confident of her own matchless and unrivalled beauty. I grow all sorts of roses, from the coppery coloured Austrian briar (*Rosa foetida*), to moss roses, to the Chinese 'Kiftsgate', with a thousand simultaneous white flowers, to the shadowless dead-pan 'Frau Karl Druschki' and the coarse, good old steadfast, pink and gold 'Peace'. The butterflies can take it or leave it, but as far as these flowers go, I am with the beetles.

The Gravel Path

The edges of garden paths, where gravel and grass meet, provide a different habitat for flowers and butterflies. Certain plants flourish exceedingly in these artificial screes.

I have found that common toadflax, heartsease and field pansy, goat's-beard, rock-roses and cinquefoils, stonecrops, flax, candytuft, forget-me-nots, pimpernels, thistles, petty spurge, daisies, thrift and so forth grow very well indeed in the no-man's-land along the edge of the path. (My thrift, which is a great lure, was ruthlessly destroyed by pigeons.) For my own amusement I have sown them with a mixture of long-headed poppies, scentless mayweed and love-in-the-mist. The poppies only attain a miniature size – say 2 inches across and 8 inches tall. The mayweed in this situation likewise grows to about 6 inches in height and the love-in-the-mist only a little more. The effect is very pretty – the same as a flowering cornfield on a Lilliputian scale. White butterflies like the mixture too, especially the candytuft and rock-roses, and a few always seem to be flitting about the edges where grass meets gravel, trying their luck here, there and everywhere. Of course red valerian seeds itself in this habitat and, curiously enough, so does old man's beard, and both are added attractions. It is delightful to have butterflies rising to meet you as you stroll along the paths. Unfortunately this type of habitat needs constant attention if it is to be kept as a scree, for the grasses and white clover and sorrels encroach at a fantastic rate, and unless you are prepared to hand weed more or less continuously you soon have an untidy green path to deal with. It is a luxury one can rarely afford except for a brief period in the spring and early summer.

The path verge is about the only place in the garden where I dare let the self-seeded creeping thistle (a species banned by the Ministry of Agriculture) grow and flower. There is no doubt it is greatly loved by butterflies, perhaps because of its delicious scent, and is sometimes in bloom when all other nectar sources seem to have failed. Moreover

it is the larval food plant of the painted lady. But in the garden it is such a dangerous plant, and once established it has to be hand dug or it soon takes over. Furthermore in old age it is no beauty. Along the edge of the path, however, it is easy to watch and control (and cut down before seeding), and it is truly a butterfly flower.

The edges of a gravel path. *1* lavender; *2* old man's beard; *3* candytuft (*Iberis umbellata*); *4* red valerian; *5* white clover; *6* field pansy; *7* creeping cinque-foil

The Hayfield in Summer

After the cowslips, come the bird's-foot trefoil – a liberal layer of scrambled eggs rather than eggs-and-bacon – and the faint memory of pale spring grass disappears in a sea of bright green. Buttercups follow and suddenly the quaking-grass is nine inches tall and the oxeye daisies are in full flower. It is the variety of plants in the hay which is so attractive. I have gradually accumulated 100 species in mine, by the simple method of collecting seed (in a paper bag) along road verges and from a nearby derelict airfield, then wire-raking a patch of the 'field' and scattering, more or less at random, the contents of the bag in the small raked patches. This is usually effective with all the clovers and vetches, and with lady's bedstraw and knapweeds. Field scabious is more capricious and after several failures I sowed these in rows in the garden and transplanted them into the field as seedlings. I did the same with harebells and ragged-robin. Of plants which I collected in this fashion I think the most attractive nectar flowers to hayfield butterflies and moths – of which the common blue is my favourite – have proved to be (1) common ragwort (which, on the Ministry of Agriculture's prohibited list, came in by itself), (2) field scabious, (3) knapweeds, (4) red clovers, (5) bird's-foot trefoil (Lepidoptera are said to take the nectar without effecting pollination), (6) campions, (7) ragged-robin, (8) yarrow, (9) thistles, (10) selfheal and bugle (the upper lip of these labiates is missing, which makes them good butterfly flowers), (11) hawkbits and cat's-ears, and (12) wild thyme (these get easily swamped by the grass). But I have seen the small white feeding in a leisurely fashion on harebells when the flowers were in a suitable position. I introduced the black-and-red burnet and cinnabar moths to this site, and both flourish. They prefer field scabious, vetches, clovers and knapweeds – if they are in bloom early enough – and ragworts.

In July last year 22 bee orchids suddenly appeared and flowered in the area, and one was found within a yard of the walls of the house.

A corner of the hayfield in summer. *1* crested dog's-tail; *2* annual meadow-grass; *3* smooth meadow-grass; *4* meadow brome; *5* perennial rye-grass; *6* meadow foxtail; *7* quaking-grass; *8* Timothy-grass; *9* rough hawkbit; *10* meadow buttercup; *11* oxeye daisy; *12* red campion; *13* lady's bed-straw; *14* common knapweed; *15* selfheal; *16* common bird's-foot trefoil; *17* dandelion

This orchid, which used to be so rare in the district (only one record up to 1940) is now quite common at Ashton. Is this plant really as capricious as it seems, or have the long cycles of our native orchids been inadequately studied? The spotted orchid also appeared unexpectedly in the lawn.

At one end, and round the borders of the hayfield, there is a fairly strong growth of grasses – the soil must be slightly different – which here attain a height of 3 feet 6 inches, and plants like the knapweeds, meadow cranes-bill and meadow vetchling are dragged up with it and grow to twice the height that they reach in short grass. There is a good mixture of grasses, but cocks-foot and Timothy were specially included as food for the brown butterflies.

I am a wildly enthusiastic grass gardener, and as the summer wears on and the stems and leaves turn a light beige in colour, the pale mauve cranes-bill, half-hidden dreamily in the straw-coloured bent grasses, seems infinitely more beautiful to me than any flower in a well-weeded bed. As you walk through the hayfield the meadow browns rise up to greet you and then settle again. Bumble-bees nest in the grass, and apart from being good pollinators themselves, the bee-flies which live as parasites in their nests are invaluable in the early spring, for with their long tongues they can feed on violets and bluebells and primroses and they are on the wing considerably before their hosts are out and about.

I try to add a few new plant species to the hayfield each year. During August 1982 I am introducing seed of the yellow rattle, and a few plants of spiny restharrow which I have grown in the kitchen garden, and some additional perforate St John's-wort. In the hayfield no two years are alike. There are good and bad years for all species of plants, due to the subtle and not so subtle but infinitely varied differences in climate – the temperature, rainfall, frost, winds, clouds, sun and so forth. This in turn affects the number of butterflies on the wing – fluctuating more dramatically and more noticeably than the plants on which they feed. In addition there is a gradual long-term evolution in the hayfield, depending to some extent, of course, on management: how often the grass is cut, with what implements, if it is baled after mowing, if it is grazed and by what animals – sheep, geese, or ponies. Change is inevitable. The art is to mould change in the direction you fancy.

I decided to try and reproduce as near as possible, but without introducing ants and anthills, a primitive Northamptonshire grass meadow in this acre of ground in 1972, so it has been developing and improving for about ten years. During the last four years the meadow brown, wall, gatekeeper, small skipper and common blue have become residents – in the sense they are breeding in the field – all but the last-named species feeding on grasses. The small elephant hawk-moths which I catch (and release) quite regularly in my light trap, also probably breed in the hayfield although I have not found their caterpillars on the masses of lady's and hedge bedstraw which perfume the whole area in July. The large elephant hawk also comes into the trap, and I am going to introduce a bit of rosebay willowherb round the edge of the field in order to encourage this beautiful moth to breed. I do not feel that the willowherb is a characteristic plant of a classical hayfield, but it is much in evidence in the derelict aerodrome a mile distant. Talk of the airfield, which is relatively an enormous unkempt area, reminds me of the question of size. How small can a hay garden be? The size is not really important for one can fill any corner with grass and wild flowers. But although a patch under an apple tree or a border framing a well cut lawn will add to the attraction of the butterfly pub, it is unlikely to suffice for any of the grass feeders as a breeding haven.

This year my field was so full of flowers I could not imagine how it could be improved, but on the other hand there were certain obvious dangers. Two menacing species of grasses had made their appearance – tor-grass and false oat-grass – and are spreading. It is not impossible that over the next five years, if left to their own devices, they could 'take over' and by their rampant growth smother the varied flora of the hayfield. No one really knows how to control tor-grass. The moment I realized it had invaded the area, I took the hard way and ploughed up the worst patches with a cultivator, and re-seeded with other grasses and flower seed. Tor-grass is still present and as menacing as ever. The late Sir Edward Salisbury, the most distinguished botanist of his day, advised close cutting and gas lime (now virtually unobtainable) for its control, but recently selective weed killers have been improved and I may experiment with Curb in a few marked-out squares of pure tor-grass. It is very easy to locate the grass, even in midwinter, since its leaves are a brighter, more metallic green than any other species of grass. Incidentally, even hungry bullocks won't graze it. I imagine it would be like eating strips of tin foil! After treatment you have to wait forty weeks before re-seeding, so ugly brown patches will disfigure the area. Irritating but unavoidable. (By the way, however practical and knowledgeable you are, you *must* follow the instructions on the weedkiller container with care and attention before use.)

How far will false oat invade? Is the soil too poor for it in the centre of the field? Can it only increase round the perimeter? It may be that the solution is to run two or three sheep round the outside of this field, for they will eat it (despite the cost and hassle of temporary fencing, be it with netting or movable electric wire) for this is a grass which is drastically reduced by grazing – no one knows why, perhaps because it does not like being trampled on.

I would like to keep my hayfield exactly as it is – but that is unlikely to happen, although I intend to try. I am enchanted with the covey of baby partridges calling somewhere in the middle of it . . . the mixture of mauve field scabious and purple knapweeds, the almost white seed heads of dried quaking-grass – even the odd hornet hunting for insect prey. On warm evenings I walk through it after dark and imagine it stretches away for thirty acres or more on all sides. In the half-light the ghost moth swings among the drying stems. It is John Clare country come back to life.

> . . . *To see the meadows so divinely lye*
> *Beneath the quiet of the evening sky.*

Grass

I have called myself a dedicated grass gardener, but so far I have only mentioned flowers which attract pollinators and ignored the grasses which are without petals or nectar and are wind pollinated – providing food only for the early stages of these insects' life-cycle. But once you are bitten by the grass bug, despite their lack of colour and scent there is no flower which seems more beautiful or graceful than wall barley or quaking-grass. And nothing is so rewarding in the garden as the hayfield 'where tides of grass break into foam of flowers'.

The grasses (Gramineae) are the most important of all the plant families, both for mankind and giant pandas. They include the cultivated cereals like wheat, maize, rice and also sugar and bamboos. Needless to say they supply food for innumerable other animals, from buffaloes to marbled whites – for 'all flesh is grass'. Furthermore the fact that most of the earth's surface from near the poles to the burning deserts and the maritime sand-dunes (not to forget the corn belts of the New World) is covered or partially covered by grasses, means that they contribute largely to one of the great miracles of all time – namely that our world is green. This is another way of saying that plants have won the silent battle against animals – for what is there otherwise to prevent voracious goats or locusts consuming every blade and leaf? Grasses are not protected by a growth of spines or thorns, nor do they produce deadly berries or a vile smell. In their case it is chiefly an effective reproductive strategy, both above and below ground, which accounts for their numerical superiority. That is why we not only eat grasses but, unconsciously, breathe them too, for during nine months of the year in England the air contains grass pollen grains and, in the spring, concentrations of 4454 grains/cm^3 have been recorded. Hay fever is a tribute to their fertility and effective system of world-wide distribution. But, practically speaking, this means you have some pretty tough customers to deal with in the garden. In any case avoid introducing strong species such as cocks-foot, tall fescue and perennial rye-grass for they are so vigorous and aggressive they will swamp just those flowers you are struggling to establish. And they will rapidly prise apart your paving stones.

Obviously if you are sowing seeds or planting seedlings into existing swards – be they ex-croquet lawns, fields or open spaces between fruit trees – you must, up to a point, accept the grasses which are already present. But you can always add different ones. I sowed quaking-grass in my hayfield with outstanding success, and also introduced the meadow foxtail, meadow barley, yellow oat-grass, crested dog's-tail, crested hair-grass, Yorkshire-fog, meadow brome, Timothy and cat's-tail. I wanted variety among the grasses, but at the same time it was necessary to consider the type of soil in my hayfield – heavy Oxford clay with little topsoil and a strong limestone element. Had I an alluvial soil I would have introduced the smooth meadow-grass for that is the most favoured species of food for the grass-eating caterpillars. Those present in my hayfield nevertheless provide nourishment for the early stages of the gatekeeper, meadow brown, small heath, wall, and speckled wood and – should I succeed in reintroducing it – the marbled white. The grass-eating brown butterflies do not seem to be very host specific and eat various grasses, many of which are not named in butterfly books.

On the derelict Polebrook airfield, only a mile away, there are grasses different from those mentioned above, including one of the relatively uncommon bush-grasses (a species of *Calamagrostis*) and several other tall, graceful species. Without bothering to identify them with certainty, I gather the seed and sprinkle it in appropriate places in the garden – along paths, in corners of the gravel courtyard and so forth. There is plenty of time to look them up in your handbook during the long winter evenings or when they are in flower next year. The bush-grass incidentally grew magnificently on the edge of the hard tennis court!

If you are planning to sow an area of bare ground with a grass and wild-flower mixture in a prepared seed bed (see p. 46) you should perhaps consider including a so-called 'nurse crop' – that is if you want to establish a quick cover of vegetation. The flowers and grasses which will form your permanent hayfield, or patch of wild flowering grass lawn, are relatively slow growing. The Nature Conservancy suggests that on my type of soil (heavy clay and limestone) you sow, together with the basic mixture, a proportion of annual Westerworlds' rye-grass (a form of *Lolium multiflorum*) which grows rapidly, and during that period of early growth protects the young flower seedlings and then dies back, giving way to the plants you wish to preserve. But it is essential to cut it before it seeds itself or it will swamp the other species. I am not much in favour of this procedure for small gardens, although it is useful for parks or extensive road verges. For the butterfly gardener I would stick to the grasses listed by the Nature Conservancy booklet *Creating Attractive Grasslands using Native Plant Species* or by seedsmen's catalogues (see Appendix), or merely those which catch your eye for their beauty and interest as you wander along the country lanes or across waste ground.

In my kitchen garden (where control is possible) I could not resist adding seeds of darnel (*Lolium temulentum*), to my patch of 'Farmer's Nightmare' (see p. 46). As a scientific experiment this is just permissable, but a serious cornfield pest of this type – or, for that matter, black bent or common couch (twitch), which are nearly as bad and could be on the banned list – should never be broadcast or disseminated, for this will bring the butterfly/wild-flower gardener into utter disrepute. For example in 1960 wild-oats were said to have cost Canadian farmers £30,000,000.

Darnel has toxic seeds – probably as a defence against seed-eating beetles, for plants are well-versed in chemical warfare. This grass was a common pest in cornfields in Elizabethan times and when accidentally ground up with wheat grains, could cause serious illness. This is what Shakespeare was referring to in *Henry VI*: '. . . Want ye corn for bread? . . . 'Twas full of darnel. Do you like the taste?' None of our butterflies feeds on it, but I grew it out of pure sentiment – because Lear not only laughed at 'gilded butterflies' but was crowned with 'cuckoo-flowers, Darnel and all the idle weeds. . .'

Most of all I love idle weeds.

Autumn in the Butterfly Garden

By September the hayfield flowers, except for a few lagging knap-weeds, are over and the butterflies have to resort to what we can offer them in the garden proper. For now we alone can supply them. This is really the moment *par excellence* for the butterfly pub. *Sedum spectabile* is in full bloom and the Michaelmas daisies – especially the old-fashioned single ones which grow in cottage gardens – are the greatest attractions. The mixture of their purple petals and the oranges of the small tortoiseshell and comma are flamboyant – almost punk. Another member of the daisy family, golden rod (which looks like anything but a daisy), is popular – with ladybirds as well as butterflies – and can be planted with advantage against a wall or fence or at the back of the herbaceous border, for it is a tall plant. Old man's beard – the really late-flowering wild clematis – has run riot in my garden – it has even seeded itself in the edge of the gravel path, and reached the roof and the top of a cherry tree. I can't resist its mass of enigmatically scented blooms, but as a butterfly attractant it cannot remotely compare with, say, *Buddleia davidii* – but that flower is over – and it is very acceptable during autumn shortages. And this is mysterious since it secretes no nectar but plenty of pollen. Do the small tortoiseshells actually consume pollen? Curiously the cultivated varieties of the meadow saffron are also sought after at this period.

This is the season when the red admirals show their predilection for over-ripe fruit. These dark angels join the wasps feeding on any plums or rotting pears left on the ground at the foot of my wall – although this year they had the fruit almost to themselves – apart from the birds. They are much more alert and wary than the specimens feeding on the Michaelmas daisies. Many Chinese artists depict swallowtail butterflies with a sharp beaky expression on their faces, and a mean look in their eyes. In the autumn red admirals have a sort of Chinese feel about them. I have seen, on two occasions, these butterflies attack hornets invading their nectar source. Usually the hornets drive them off. What do we know of their private lives? Very little I would say. A section of the population, of course, dies of old age in the autumn and a relatively small number creep into a bark crevice high up on some towering tree trunk, or under ivy, and hibernate successfully. The majority migrate southwards after their orgy on fruit juices, navigating by reference to the position of the sun, lead lines and the strength and direction of the wind. One moonlit night in the early autumn, when the garden was swathed in a low-lying silvery mist, I ran a mercury vapour moth lamp, and to my great astonishment, in the morning, found it chock-a-block with sleeping red admirals. This suggested that these butterflies also migrate on moonlit nights – and the southbound stream had been misled by my lamp seen through the fog. These travellers, when they reach their unknown destination, probably in southern Europe or north Africa, either breed during the winter or the next spring. By the following June to August they, or their offspring, arrive back in our gardens to join the resident red admirals.

The unstable English weather produces strains of both butterflies and birds with mixed resident and migrant populations. Swedish woodpigeons, for example, all migrate south in winter, but, like the red admirals, in the British Isles some of our birds remain behind, and are the first to breed in the spring before the migrants return. In fact our weather selects genes for various sorts of hedging bets.

What role does the butterfly's eyesight play in migration? What does the English Channel look like to a red admiral on its way to our gardens? We can only guess. It is a strange fact that all animals – butterflies, pigs, clams, fish, fleas, whales, shrews and shrimps – all see by virtue of yellow pigments – carotenoids – which they obtain directly from plants, or indirectly from other animals which have eaten plants. Rhodopsin, the visual pigment, is derived (via Vitamin A) from carotenoids – and no animals can manufacture it for themselves. We depend on plants for the gift of vision; without green leaves we would all be blind. Carotenoids are very mysterious. Why are there 300 known different kinds, and why does the large white store 17 of them and the swallowtail only three? We simply haven't a clue. The slug-like caterpillars of the common blue look green and merge in with the seeds and tiny leaves of their food plant, because the yellow carotenoids and blue bile pigments present in their body tissues mix in the eye of the beholder, and make their resulting green camouflage near perfect. You can, nowadays, rear these butterflies on artificial diets lacking carotenoids, and then – because they secrete their own bile pigments – they are sky blue in colour, not leaf green. But the azure of the common blue's wings is due to light reflected off the ridges on their scales.

Heliotrope, which has to be planted out in early summer, and blooms until the first touch of frost blackens it, is a tremendous attraction for the butterflies. This flower, as we have seen, smells strongly of vanilla, but it also contains in its foliage chemicals known as pyrrolizidine alkaloids. These are poisonous to vertebrates, producing cancer of the liver, blood diseases, etc., but, in the lives of butterflies and moths, play very different and important roles. The cinnabar moth, for instance, which obtains these substances from the caterpillars' food plant, ragworts, stores them in its body tissues as a protection against the attack of various predators, for their taste is bitter and caustic, and their effect after ingestion painful and stressful. Most birds and spiders leave them alone after the initial experience. But in tropical countries certain male butterflies ingest the chemicals with the juices or sap of wilting plants like heliotrope, and then use them as an ingredient of their sex attractants. They possess bunches of abdominal hairs and from these they shake derivatives of the pyrrolizidines, in the form of a cloud of minute particles, over the female. This scented 'love dust' immediately overcomes her natural coyness: she is arrested in flight, bewitched . . . copulation ensues. Strangely enough these chemicals are also found in the nectar of ragworts and possibly butterflies which feed on them may also find protection as well as food. Usually plants do not incorporate any potent chemicals in nectar for they don't want to risk harming prospective pollinators.

The ivy comes into bloom late in September, and is all that is left to draw the red admirals which are still around. Every fly and every bee left in the garden settles on the globular flowerheads with their powerful, sickly, almost foetid scent – often joined by the odd hornet. It is an awesome buzzing conglomeration. On the Island of Rhodes at the end of September the thousands of red and cream-coloured Jersey tiger moths, which aestivate in the so-called Valley of the Butterflies, take their first nectar meal after their long summer fast from the ivy blossoms festooning the trees. From May until September they live on their accumulated fat reserves, cooling themselves by sitting on the damp rocks, only drinking the water trickling down the waterfall into the stream which runs through the valley. It is an unforgettable sight to see them bejewelling the ivy – as if the whole tree had burst into a mass of scarlet and yellow flowers. Unfortunately the Jersey tiger is exceedingly rare in Britain and you are unlikely to entice it into the garden, unless you live in South Devon where you might be lucky.

One or two painted lady butterflies may also visit the ivy blossom in late September. These butterflies are powerful migrants, flying south for 2–3000 kilometres, leaving Britain at the end of August. If your garden is large enough some males may establish a home-range or a 'territory', patrolling the area they have selected and chasing off any other butterfly which enters their airspace. In China I once saw large black swallowtails chasing small birds out of their territory. Peacock butterflies also establish territories, but usually not in small gardens – just as the regular, if casual pub-crawler feels no sense of ownership about the Crown and Anchor or the King's Head.

The early autumn is the time for the grass gardener to transplant his seedlings into existing sward. After the first mow about mid-September (see next chapter) you can put in the young cowslips, ragged-robin, field scabious, buttercups – in fact all those plants you have grown for the purpose in rows in beds, frames or trays. It is a good plan to broadcast a few seeds of the same species where you plant the seedlings. Before doing this, check the acidity and alkalinity of your soil. It may have changed, and if you are grass gardening on Oxford clay or a similar type of soil, add some lime, for the pH for wild flowers in this habitat should not fall below 7–8. It is also the moment for sowing your wild flower seed in the kitchen garden. You need a well-dug soil, free of weeds, reduced to a fine firm seed bed. Do not use manure or fertilizer. So far I've treated most species as if they were carrots, digging a small furrow and sowing the seed by hand and raking back the soil.

With the seeds of wild flowers one may be faced with germination problems. Thus some seeds, like cowslip, require a period of cold treatment – exposure to a near-freezing temperature in the fridge for between 1 to 6 weeks – if they are to be sown in pans in a standard seed compost of three parts peat, one part loam and one part grit (by bulk, not weight). Various vetches and clovers need prolonged exposure to leaching by rain and the soil solution to remove the germination inhibitors in their seed coats, while others again, germinate more successfully after scarification (rubbing between sandpaper). Obviously if seeds are sown outside, special treatments are unnecessary. However, the problems encountered are more subtle than this. We are ignorant of the ideal conditions conducive to good germination, and without being aware of them we can intitiate dormancy in our seeds by unknown adverse circumstances. I have no idea what I did to my oxeye daisy seeds last season, but they failed to germinate for several months after planting. This year's seeds, from the same parent plants, apparently with the same treatment, germinated within a week to ten days. A single white clover plant can produce 85% of seed which germinates within a year, but the rest may lie dormant up to 20 years. But in some circumstances 90% of the seeds are forced into dormancy. In nature this can be useful, for the risks are spread by temporal diversity. The burnet moth caterpillar, by sometimes going into aestivation (summer 'hibernation' following true hibernation in winter) achieves the same purpose, thus in a certain proportion of the population, the developmental period is spread over two years.

The wild-flower gardener must be prepared for such unforeseen eventualities – for we know so little about buttercups and daisies! On the other hand we need never give up hope. One year I thought my cowslip seed could be written off as a complete failure because the initial germination test gave a rate of 3 per cent; three months later it proved to be 97 per cent.

In all probability you will buy your wild flower seed from a well-known seedsman like John Chambers or Suffolk Herbs (read the instructions on the packet carefully!), but you may decide to gather your own either from your garden or from some road verge or waste ground. (Even so, you must be careful not to rob rare species.) In this case considerable care, a lot of common garden-sense and some knowledge of wild flowers is useful.

First of all it is quite difficult to find the plants in the autumn which you mentally marked down for seed gathering in the spring. Thus in March you may have been thrilled by a mass of snowy white violets along the bank of a deep roadside ditch, and returned in the early autumn to gather a little seed. But you find the site transformed. The bank is covered in coarse vegetation – a tangle of grasses, nettles, huge leaves of hogweed and so forth. You can't find the violets at all – let alone the seeds. Much the same applies to the cowslips and buttercups which you saw in such profusion in a particular spot in the spring. When the seed is ripe – late summer and early autumn – they are difficult to find and quite often some knowing bird – the avian variety – has been there before you. Nor does seed ripen all at once. In damp sites cowslip seed should be harvested as much as a month later than those in open, dry situations like chalk downland or well-drained sunbaked grassfields. You have to judge the situation intuitively. For good germination the seeds should ripen before gathering, but you can't afford to leave it too long – until a rainstorm knocks them out or the ants carry them off. Not only does the site affect the time of ripening but there is an enormous genetic variation in this character. Thus, for example, if you want an early flowering oxeye daisy, you should gather your seed from those which flower first, for the chances are that those are an early flowering mini-strain and their offspring will follow suit.

The brief time during which wild flowers are in bloom is a grief to the butterfly gardener, and to increase the span of flowering you want to select seed from plants which are 'out' both early and late. Thus seed gathering is also spread over quite a long period and unless you are a professional there is a tendency to leave it too late. When the flowers are in bloom you are full of good intentions – but there is always too much to do in the garden and so little time in the evenings and at weekends. The luncheon interval is best for seed gathering – for then the dew has evaporated and it is very good for your figure, too, for sooner or later you drop the sandwiches and lose the bag. It is as well to dry seed for a few days after gathering, for a certain amount of ripening can take place on a sheet of paper in a sunny window.

Winter in the Butterfly Garden and the Hayfield

It is a fact that in England butterflies are recorded from every month of the year, and on a sunny winter day small tortoiseshells not infrequently make a mistake and creep out of some crack or roof space where they have been hibernating and sun themselves in the inhospitable garden. I once saw such a butterfly plunge back into a pile of logs where no doubt it had been sound asleep for the last four months. Peacocks, when aroused from sleep, sometimes make quite audible clicking noises. No one knows how they do it.

The butterfly flowers and creepers you planted for their spring and summer nectar sometimes have fine fruits which enhance the winter garden. The black and red berries of the wayfaring tree, the purple sloes, the scarlet or yellow fruit of the holly, the shocking pink and orange berries of the spindle, and the hips and haws adorn the hedges. When the first frost occurs the holly's leaves are scalloped in rime and look extraordinarily beautiful. Old man's beard, with its persistent styles which grow out into long feathery awns, makes the best hoar frost photos of them all. As I have said, this wild clematis has run riot over one end of my house, and on an icy winter morning I can look out at a white world through a window framed in delicate glittering curls.

The crucial management problems of the grass gardener really arise in the late autumn rather than the winter, but they span both seasons. With a view to encouraging the maximum growth and flowering of the wild species, when must one mow? And how will this affect the developmental stages of the butterflies? None of us has enough experience to give a categorical answer, but my own ten years of grass gardening has resulted in a rough rule of thumb: the moment there are no more flowers in the hayfield, I cut the grass.

This is usually during the first two weeks of September, for up to then there is a good show of knapweeds, and the blues are still in evidence in the field.

I confess that by this time I am ready to cut the grass – both the hayfield and the bank. It is brown and hairy and rain sodden and the dogs have flattened it in the most conspicuous areas in front of the house; in fact it has become unmanageable. There is no doubt that shorn of their straggling tresses, the lawns look smooth, neat and rather smug, even if a little colourless. The crab apples, 'Hornet' and other varieties, are loaded with golden fruit and stand out against it like a Cellini jewelled model. 'Nothing is more pleasant to the eye', said Francis Bacon, 'than green grass kept finely shorn'. After September mowing it will take about three weeks for my lawn to become really green again.

If it is warm and wet during October, or for some other reason the grass grows strongly, I mow a second time in the early part of November. This is a relatively trivial task. There is a small part of my garden which I cut in the spring. By doing this I lose the flowers of a number of plants such as quaking-grass, but on the other hand a variety of species like thistles, ragwort, bird's-foot trefoil, lady's bedstraw, selfheal, knapweeds, some buttercups, centauries, etc., will then flower very late, and provide a nectar source well into early October. This section is not mown in the early autumn.

The cut grass is removed from the garden on a tractor, but it should first be left for a few days to allow any young caterpillars to crawl down into the remains of their food plants. It is then spread in an adjoining grass field in an attempt to re-create a similar area by this method of seed dispersal. If there is time, hand threshing on a large plastic sheet retrieves a certain amount of seed. If the cut grass is left on the field it has a deleterious effect after three months on the following year's 'crop', and if no other method is practical and there are no farm animals to feed, a smouldering bonfire in one corner is the answer. For the sake of larval butterflies I always leave one bank uncut – but I have a very large garden so this is not a serious problem on the score of untidiness. In the spring, daffodils in uncut grass which is still dry and light brown in colour can be very attractive, though not to everyone's taste.

As I mentioned on p. 33, this year I intend to tackle the tor-grass problem by introducing selective weed killers to the butterfly hayfield. Since tor-grass can extinguish all the other desirable plants it is probably the lesser of two evils, though intuitively I am anti-herbicide. There is, however, a different approach where you wish to substitute any area of ground with unwanted grasses or weeds for an attractive flowering meadow or patch of grass with wild flowers growing in it. Don't attempt to plant into existing sward. Be ruthless: start from scratch. In the first place cut the grass or weeds short with an Allen Autoscythe and then go over it once again with a Hayter Rotary Mower. Remove the cuttings and rotovate the area. Then treat it with a weed killer such as Roundup.

After Roundup you need only wait two to three weeks. Then prepare a good seed bed by cultivating the area, breaking the soil down to a fine tilth by harrowing or hoeing (and rolling in the case of light soils) with the tools appropriate to the size of the area. You should then lime the seed bed according to the pH of the soil, but at all costs avoid fertilizers. Purchase a grass or wild-flower seed mixture from one of the few merchants (see appendix) who provide the mixtures suggested by the Nature Conservancy (see p. 37), first telling them the type of soil found in your garden – whether it can be described as heavy, clay, alluvial, sandy, chalky or limestone.

It is best to consult the seedsman about the quantity required. You should also ask him to add any wild flowers you particularly fancy not listed in the mixture he is proposing. You should also ask for the addition of my own packet called the 'Farmer's Nightmare'. This is not recommended by the Nature Conservancy in their booklet, but it has proved very successful in small areas, say half an acre downwards. I think it preferable to a grass nurse crop (see p. 36). This 'nightmare' mixture contains mayweeds, poppies, cornflowers, corncockles, corn marigolds, oats and barley, which only flower the first year of seeding while the main crop is relatively sparse and there are patches of bare arable soil available. The perennial wild flowers often delay blooming until the following year. Once the grass mixture has begun to grow strongly there is too much competition for the poppies, cornflowers and the other annuals (which usually grow in cornfields) and they will disappear after adding great beauty to the initial year's growth, which can otherwise prove disappointingly short of colour. Someone who followed this recipe described her first year grass plot as a Claude Monet come to life.

Almost all the gardeners I know who have started from 'scratch' in the way described above have found that, despite the weed killer, weeds such as thistles or fat-hen have somehow come in and established themselves happily in their grass and wild-flower mixture. Very interesting! There is only one practical method of dealing with this problem in a small garden where the area planted is not more than half an acre in extent: grit your teeth and hand weed early. Thistles can blow in from miles away; fat-hen can lay dormant in the soil for 35 years and then germinate successfully in arable soil. Neither can be tolerated, however much you admire their adaptation to life, and hand weeding is the answer. If the area you wish to re-seed is growing a mixture of the more usual grasses – and not the very aggressive species like Yorkshire-fog, or tor-grass – ploughing-in may be preferable to using herbicides, or you can disc- or chain-harrow the seeds in to a close-cut existing sward.

If you have a kitchen garden of your own and can spare the time, you can grow the species of wild flowers you wish to add subsequently to your flowering grass area (see the preceding chapter).

Winter is the time for clearing-up, trimming, judicious removals, cutting-out dead wood, digging, experimenting, planning, remembering and day-dreaming in front of a log fire! I remember catching a swallowtail in my garden . . . high summer, rolling white clouds, a ground mist of Queen Anne's lace. (Perhaps the Queen Anne's lace has got out of hand? – No, the swallowtail had not escaped from Syon House or been blown over from France; it was the British subspecies. Nor was it a long-distance pub crawler. It had hatched from a chrysalis in a fresh consignment of Norfolk reed which had been used for re-thatching a tool shed . . .) It is four o'clock and dusk is falling very rapidly. The books tell you that elm logs only smoulder . . . wrong again . . . How will this icy spell affect the tiny common blue butterfly and burnet caterpillars hibernating near the mown grass roots? They must be frozen as hard as pebbles. Or do they secrete anti-freeze? Will there be snow storms of whites next year or just one ragged peacock among the cherry blossom? The flames from the elm logs whisk up the chimney like birds of paradise chasing small coppers. Yes, there *must* be a glitter of small coppers round the dock and charlock next spring. I had almost forgotten the charlock seed . . . near the cross roads . . . on the verge . . .

What do Butterflies See?

It appears highly probable that butterflies, like ourselves, 'seem naturally attracted to give special attention to all coloured substances'.

In the garden we should be able to plan to please the small copper and blues as well as ourselves. But what do butterflies SEE?

It is not possible to describe the colour red to a man blind from birth. It is almost as difficult to try and imagine what the sky looks like to, say, a large white, since, unlike you or me it can see polarized light – that is to say the light waves vibrating at right angles to the direction in which they are travelling. If we were standing at the bottom of a deep well at midday with only a small patch of blue sky visible, we might look upwards and see the odd star shining, but we could not tell the direction of the sun. But a butterfly could do so – for the rays of polarized light indicate the sun's position – a sort of sun compass. But what does it all *look* like? Does the sky seem slatted to a large white – alternate lines of bright light and shade, like a Venetian blind or the old Japanese flag – or does it seem darker blue/green away from the sun, or is the vault of heaven dismembered into sectors that differ in colour or intensity? Does this pattern shift relative to the butterfly as its line of vision or its direction of flight changes? Should we think of it as another unimaginable sort of colour vision? Like many other things we simply do not know.

There are, however, some aspects of insect eyes and insect vision which can be tested by observation and experiment. We know, for instance, that butterflies' eyes, which bulge outwards from their heads, are made up of thousands of separate lenses (ommatidia) set closely together and so arranged that the butterfly can see all around itself – not just forward – without turning its head. The large white's world must seem like a well-lit bowl. Also the lenses in the bottom half of many insects' eyes are different from the rest – specialized for close-up vision. In fact they provide natural bifocals. Sometimes these 'bifocals' only see colour in the bottom half – the top sees the world as a black and white film.

Butterflies can see more colours than we do. Perhaps their appreciation of the red end of the spectrum is not as good as ours but, unlike us, at the opposite end they see into the ultra violet. (In fact it is with their ultra-violet receptors that they can appreciate polarized light.) This means that many flowers which seem uniformly coloured to us, like for instance the glossy yellow lesser celandine, if photographed by an ultra-violet camera, reveal dark nectar guides round the centre. These petal guide-lines – so often invisible to us – assist a flying insect to find the spot where the nectar is stored, suggesting they tend to be short-sighted. Flowers which are pollinated by humming birds, which have marvellously acute long sight, are not provided with nectar guides. Many male butterflies signal to their females with the aid of ultra violet, which, as they flap their wings, glances off their especially structured scales like tiny flashes of lightning.

There are no butterflies in Britain with transparent wings, although some moths lose their wing scales after emergence. These insects can probably signal by means of polarized light, for the scaleless wing veins glow like molten gold if viewed under a microscope with the appropriate polarizing filters.

Some biologists believe that moths can sense the individual infra-red patterns emitted by plants in the dark. We ourselves are conscious of the infra-red reflection in photographs of bluebell woods, since the beautiful azure tint is lost and, due to the sensitivity of the photographic emulsion on the film to infra red, they appear a rather disappointing mauve. Butterflies probably see these flowers a brighter blue colour than even we do, since they are less sensitive to the longer waves of light. For this reason you would expect poppies to be less exciting to insects than they are to us; but, apart from their red colour, they relfect ultra violet and the effect must be greatly accentuated by the crinkled petals, so that they – presumably – shine and flash as they shake in the breeze. A number of species, however, do not see red at all, and to them the beautiful scarlet poppies would look black with a silver glance.

None will deny that colour rather than shape attracts the ordinary gardener to his flowers. Perfectly shaped the rose 'Étoile de Hollande' may be, but it would lose much of its attraction if it were the same shade as the leaves. Butterflies, like us, rate colour above outline. From a distance the flower border is a blur of lovely shades and subtle tones and brilliant patches of coloured light, and we both fail to distinguish individual shapes and sizes, but the distant view of flowers has a special attraction, like the *fata Morgana*. Once, a chance visitor to my bluebell wood, on catching sight of this wonderful azure sea, stripped naked and plunged in among the flowers. This struck a casual passer-by as extraordinarily eccentric. But was it? The passing small tortoiseshell butterfly may also be overcome by the blue perfumed air, and sink in ecstasy among the serried ranks of ultramarine bells.

To appeal to a butterfly's eye, stands of flowers are better than single ones, and the finest combination is yellow and mauve with a sweet scent. Robert Bridges thought that if odour were visible as colour he would see the summer garden aureoled in rainbow clouds. It is easy to imagine that the butterflies on a summer afternoon are caught up in a golden bowl of light in which scent and colour are inextricably mixed.

Suddenly, when the eggs begin to develop in her oviducts, the female large white's colour preference undergoes a dramatic change. Blue, purple, red and yellow cease to attract her. She has an eye only for green – cabbage green. Incidentally the different shades of green one sees in foliage never cease to astonish me and I believe they are developed as part of plant strategy against insect herbivores. They are no accident of time and space.

As far as egg-laying is concerned, once the large white has become hooked on cabbage green she turns her attention to plant chemistry and tests all the attractive leaves for the presence of mustard oils. Then she lays. But the colour must be right. Red cabbage and variegated cabbage leaves are studiously ignored. Males may sometimes follow the female to your vegetable garden, but usually remain among the lavender bushes, sipping nectar. Once the female has laid her eggs her lust for green cabbage leaves vanishes as suddenly as it came, and she returns in a flirtatious mood to the lavender and her male companions. This is another reason why rape should be treated like a border flower, for the leaves will appease the white butterflies when they develop an eye for cabbage green, and will prevent them wandering off into your vegetable garden and beyond, when the desperate need to fulfil their maternal instincts overwhelms them.

Will Butterflies Stay?

No less a hero than Sir Winston Churchill tried and failed to persuade butterflies to breed in his garden, and Denis Owen, a professional entomologist, found that only the large and small white, and perhaps the orange tip, bred in his – the other thirteen species he noted regarded it as a temporary home. On the other hand, by a process of capture, marking and then releasing butterflies, he showed that in a period of five years no less than 9000 individual specimens passed through his 658 m² of suburban (Leicestershire) garden – attracted, so he concluded, by the 230 or more species of flowering plants (120 foreign) he had planted there.

But despite the fact that he also introduced the foodplant (stinging nettle) of the small tortoiseshell – the commonest visitors apart from the whites – they did not breed. I have been considerably more fortunate myself, but I am confident this is due to the fact that my garden is large (four acres) and at one end adjoins a woodland nature reserve, and since I have created a hayfield in the garden it has virtually become an extension or spill-over from the nature reserve itself. Fortunately the small tortoiseshell, peacock, small copper, holly blue, common blue, wall, meadow brown, gatekeeper and small heath, and the large and small skippers have all bred in the garden at one time or another. However, I have never tried to introduce butterflies by catching them – say on the derelict airfield – and putting them out on flowers during hours of darkness in my garden, hoping that when they awake in the morning they will stay. Nor have I released pairs *in cop.*, or females about to lay eggs. Nor have I reared caterpillars in breeding cages or confined them in muslin 'sleeves' on trees and then released the adults when they had passed through the chrysalis stage. I have concentrated entirely on creating a flowery habitat that they will enjoy.

On the other hand, five brightly coloured day-flying moths, colonial in habit and therefore more static, have been introduced successfully and have now bred for several consecutive years in the garden. First choice was the cinnabar moth, which as a caterpillar feeds on ragworts. Several hundred larvae were collected from a field in this district and placed in batches of twenty on separate plants of fairly tall, flowering ragwort. A large number were taken by wasps, but a small colony was established successfully. The next two moths which 'did' extremely well were the five- and six-spot burnets. Cocoons were collected from a lay-by on the A421 near Bicester and directly they hatched and pairs formed, were released at dusk onto the meadow vetchling in the garden. Quite a sizeable colony has built up in the hayfield during the past three years, although the moths have changed onto other food plants and now feed on bird's-foot trefoil and various clovers, as well as the meadow vetchling, and tend to make their cocoons nearer the ground. Has this got something to do with mowing the grass in autumn? I noticed the same change of habit when I previously established a new colony of burnets in Oxfordshire on a lawn, and I have a hunch this may not be a good sign in the long run. We can but watch events.

The fourth moth I established, with the help of the late Bernard Kettlewell, was the scarlet tiger. He had planted a comfrey in his own garden near Oxford and had kept a flourishing colony of this moth going for about fifteen years. We planted the same species (*Symphytum caucasicum*) in the garden at Ashton and, when the plant was growing vigorously, transferred some young larvae to the leaves. The scarlet tiger, unlike the cinnabar and the burnets, is not found in Northamptonshire – it is a 'native' of the southern counties of England and there is an important difference between our climate and that of Oxfordshire, where the moth is not uncommon in circumscribed areas. It is a golden rule both for wild flowers and insects that one should only try and grow or breed those which naturally 'do well' in your district, and which are consequently quite easy to find both as larvae and adults. There is a world of difference between an introduction and a re-introduction. Finally I collected a fair number of magpie moth caterpillars, nearly full grown, and let them out on my gooseberry bushes. They flourished exceedingly and I can only hope this moth keeps going. It is a beautiful insect with its yellow body and black and white wings, and, like Gerald Manley Hopkins, I have a corny love for dappled and freckled things . . .

Some species in nature, like the black hairstreak, breed on the same blackthorn bushes for decade after decade. For over a hundred years they have been feeding on the identical bushes in the nature reserve at Ashton – refusing stubbornly to shift to the mass of new plants put in for their benefit. On the other hand my impression is that a great many species are not conservative, and from one season to another in nature, shift their breeding grounds even if only for short distances. For this reason, if for no other, a large garden is needed if you want to persuade butterflies to take up residence, rather than just drop in.

The Lepidoptera have countless enemies, from viruses to sparrows. But in my garden I fear wasps more than birds. They are voracious hunters of the caterpillar stage, and the elimination of wasp nests is of primary importance. The rough type of gardening that I indulge in here suits wasps, and in 1980 I destroyed 126 nests within a 50-yard radius of the house – all of them situated in holes in long grass. My son, aged eight, thought he could make his fortune rearing garden tigers on groundsel in the open. In this case ants dissipated his dreams of untold millions.

The more specimens you attract to your flowers, the more likely it is that some will breed, but not in the immediate vicinity of the nectar source. A large garden will not necessarily suit them, but a small one almost certainly will not. You get some idea of the space they require if you decide to follow a large white about to lay her eggs. You will need to be something of an athlete – preferably a steeplechase runner – for she is extremely hard to please, and will investigate a large number of potentially suitable plants on which her offspring could feed and breed, sometimes flying really rapidly between stops. You may have to run a mile or more, and climb over the kitchen garden wall and then unexpectedly and hurriedly climb back again before she finally selects the plant to which she confides her golden eggs.

It is fairly obvious that in the garden the large, colourful butterflies are most in evidence in the summer and early autumn. But these are specimens which will go into hibernation, migrate to warmer climates, or die of old age. The time when the butterflies will be breeding and producing their first brood is in the spring when they are much less conspicuous. The cherry blossom and the sallow catkins, the colt's foot, the alyssum and dames-violet must attract the small tortoiseshells, peacocks and orange tips if you want them to lay naturally on your nettles, lady's smock and garlic mustard (or Jack-by-the-hedge). For the grass feeders and vetch feeders, like the browns and the blues, which pass their winter as tiny caterpillars, the breeding season is, of course, much later (see Appendix).

Following pages, a suggested design for a butterfly garden, which includes many nectar and caterpillar foodplants

53

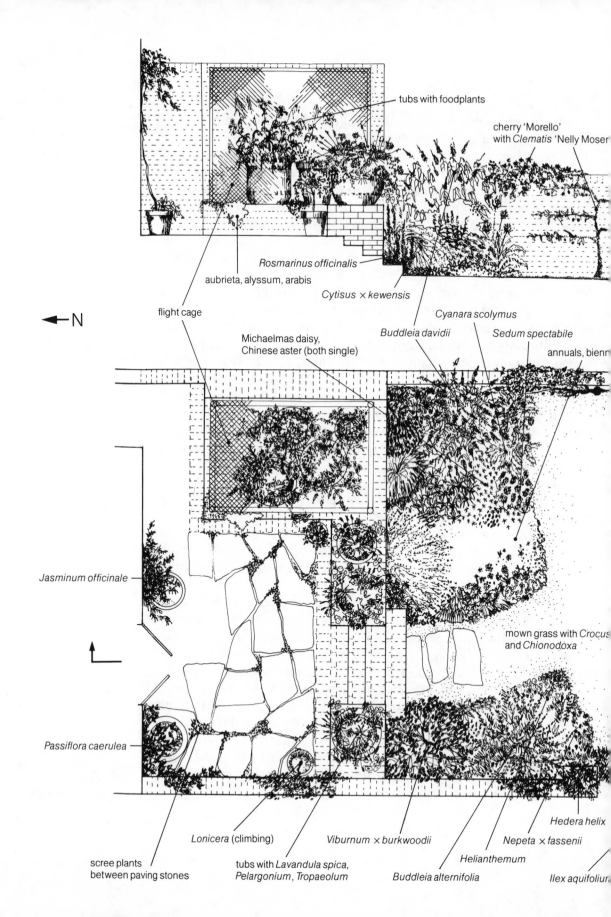

tubs with foodplants

cherry 'Morello' with *Clematis* 'Nelly Moser'

Rosmarinus officinalis

aubrieta, alyssum, arabis

Cytisus × *kewensis*

← N

flight cage

Cyanara scolymus

Michaelmas daisy, Chinese aster (both single)

Buddleia davidii

Sedum spectabile

annuals, bienn

Jasminum officinale

mown grass with *Crocus* and *Chionodoxa*

Passiflora caerulea

Hedera helix

Lonicera (climbing)

Viburnum × *burkwoodii*

Nepeta × *fassenii*

scree plants between paving stones

tubs with *Lavandula spica*, *Pelargonium*, *Tropaeolum*

Helianthemum

Buddleia alternifolia

Ilex aquifoliur

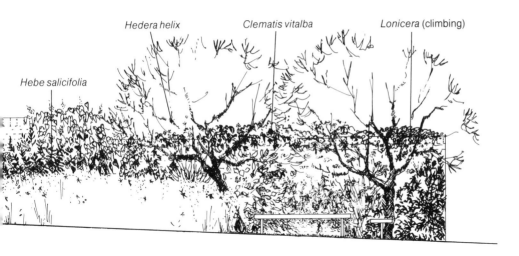

Hebe salicifolia *Hedera helix* *Clematis vitalba* *Lonicera* (climbing)

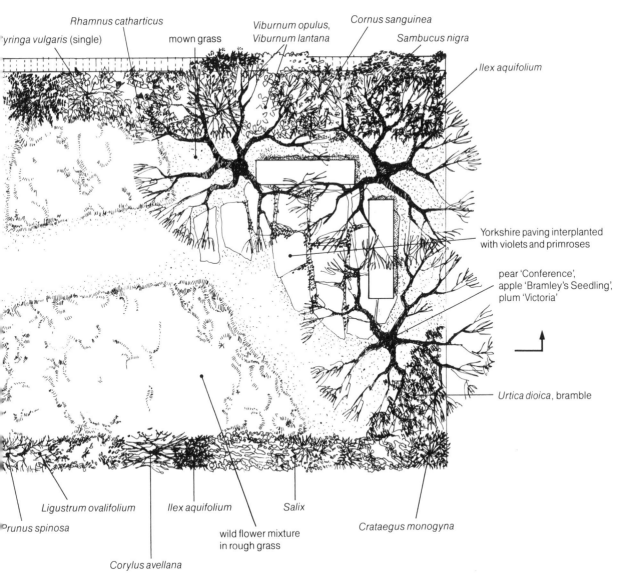

Syringa vulgaris (single) *Rhamnus catharticus* mown grass *Viburnum opulus, Viburnum lantana* *Cornus sanguinea* *Sambucus nigra* *Ilex aquifolium*

Yorkshire paving interplanted with violets and primroses

pear 'Conference', apple 'Bramley's Seedling', plum 'Victoria'

Urtica dioica, bramble

Prunus spinosa *Ligustrum ovalifolium* *Ilex aquifolium* *Salix* *Crataegus monogyna*

Corylus avellana wild flower mixture in rough grass

In this day and age one is lucky to have any help at all in the garden, even with mowing, unless, of course, you are attached to a botanical department at a large university, or a garden centre, or a nursery-man. Therefore it is virtually impossible to find the time both to garden and breed butterflies. But if by some lucky chance you can collaborate with a butterfly breeder like my co-author, a more elaborate attempt can be made, both to entice the passing butterflies in, and also to persuade them to stay and breed. There are certain plants which grow in warmer climates than ours, such as *Lantana*, a bush of the verbena family, which is extraordinarily attractive to a great variety of butterflies, many of them outside its normal distribution range. It has to be grown in a heated greenhouse but in summer it can be temporarily planted out in the garden or sunk in its own pot in the ground. The same applies to *Verbena bonariensis* – a plant about 2 to 3 feet high with bluish flowers – which vies with *Buddleia* for popularity. Again, the South African plant *Pentas*, which also needs to be grown under glass, is intensely attractive to both butterflies and moths and can be planted out during the summer. Some of the asclepiad plants like the wax flower and *Stephanotis* are also more attractive than most of our native species and, in fact, if you can draw on a greenhouse collection geared for butterflies like that described by Clive Farrell later in this book, you can double the lure of the summer season in your garden.

So much for the pub, but what about the residence? Of course it is essential to provide the right foodplant for the caterpillars, and for the female to lay on. But this is not so difficult, for out of the probable visitors to the garden, three species of white and the orange tip feed on the common plants of the cabbage family, five of the brilliantly coloured nymphalids feed on stinging nettle (the painted lady also on thistles), while six of the rest, the blues, browns and skippers, eat grasses. There are single feeders on holly, dock and buckthorn, but none of these plants presents any serious problem.

The next step is to breed the butterflies you wish to establish. It is better to start with only two species and to select the commonest and those which visit your garden – probably the small tortoiseshell and the peacock. In any case you should never collect rare species – for whatever purpose. What you really need is a flight cage – in other words a fruit cage (the size is of course dictated by the size of your garden but a minimum of 6 feet high × 8 feet square is necessary), over-covered in really fine black nylon net. It must have shelter from the wind, and some shade. Inside the cage you want a good stand of stinging nettles; some of these should be cut down to produce a succession of young shoots. If you are a bit of an entomologist you will have no difficulty in finding a brood of small tortoiseshell caterpillars and peacocks during the summer in the wild, for they are conspicuous, self-advertising objects on the nettles. Take the whole brood back in a plastic bag and release them in your flight cage onto the nettles. They will, in all probability, feed up without difficulty and pupate, either on vegetation or in a corner of the cage. This larval stage lasts 20–40 days and the chrysalis stage another two weeks. If you can't find any caterpillars yourself, purchase them from a dealer like Worldwide Butterflies. If you can afford it, it is more satisfactory to purchase your stock at the chrysalis stage (but they are about three times more expensive than eggs, say, in 1983, 40p each) or as larvae. Should you become hooked on breeding British butterflies or the large hawk moths, you can extend your range of foodplants or butterfly species, again purchasing your stock from dealers.

The easiest butterfly flowers to grow in the flight cage are dandelions and ragworts. By judicious cutting you can keep the ragwort blooming until October. But it is necessary to produce a series of good butterfly pot plants to move into the flight cage when required – and here you must once again obtain the assistance of your butterfly breeder, unless you are lucky enough to have a heated greenhouse and another pair of hands to help you with the growing of the right succession of suitable blooms, once the chrysalids have hatched. If the butterflies are kept in the flight cage for a few days after emerging and then released, by leaving the door open, they are less inclined to disperse. Paul Whalley and the late Hugh Newman, great experts in the butterfly world, both suggested this is the most hopeful way of getting the common species to take up residence. Hugh Newman stressed the importance of an ivy-covered shed in which the small tortoiseshells and peacocks could subsequently hibernate. Most people are too lazy to mark their releases, so cannot be sure if their insects stay with them, merging in with the visitors on the *Buddleia* only for the time being, or if they, too, eventually move on with the pub crawlers. If you are seduced by butterflies and can afford the time, there is no triumph greater than establishing them securely in your own garden. But the average gardener, especially if he has no professional breeder to work with him, must be satisfied with his role of enthusiastic and generous publican.

Making New Habitats
and Creating Butterfly Flowers

About eighty years ago it was first realized that attempting to conserve individual rare species was poor conservation. What was required was the preservation of a piece of natural countryside, whether meadow, mountain or woodland, where the species in question thrived. This automatically preserved the physical features, such as soil or rock formation, the right atmospheric conditions and other plants and animals which characterized the area where the rare species was found – the habitat. Since then conservationists all over the world have adopted the habitat strategy and have attempted to conserve animal and plant communities presenting special features of interest, not only because of the rare species present, but as an interacting community in varying situations and conditions. Recently, however, the International Union for the Conservation of Nature has pointed out that the destruction and modification of natural habitats has continued at such a pace that it has now become imperative to *re-create* habitats for both the fast disappearing flora and fauna, and to conserve 'off site' as well as 'on site', that is *outside* their natural surroundings.

It is, of course, totally impossible to rebuild even a relatively simple community – the result of eons of evolution – exactly as it was before destruction. Thus Professor Mellanby suggests that it would take 1000 years to reconstruct a 'primitive' Northamptonshire grassland, but it is extremely doubtful if even then it could be wholly successful . . . Nevertheless, as I know from experience, one can produce a superficially good imitation in ten years. And there is no doubt that this rather naive experiment could be vastly improved, with knowledge and experience. Thus, for instance, large hard ant hills were a great feature of Northamptonshire primitive grassland, so much so that to gallop across a field round Ashton on a pony was a hazardous enterprise. Ants are not only important pollinators, but they also play a significant role in seed dispersal. They should almost certainly be introduced into my hayfield. The re-creation of habitat reserves, however, must be the concern of professional or specialist conservationists, not of those of us who cultivate wild flowers for pure pleasure, or to attract blue butterflies.

There are one or two important points to remember in connection with growing wild flowers in gardens and parks, and along highways. Firstly, concentrate on the common species, especially those which are declining, owing to drainage and other aspects of intensive agriculture. The cowslip is the best known example. It is an error to cultivate rare species, for this creates the temptation to filch them from the wild. Secondly, wholesale gathering of wild seed should be discouraged at all levels from school teachers to local authorities. The moment a new enterprise becomes of commercial interest, or financially profitable, people will go to great lengths to participate in the bonanza. Dealers on the continent have been known to give a six-week training course to seed gatherers and then send them out in teams to collect on a massive scale. A moment's reflection will show you that seed collecting in this fashion is quite as deleterious to the native flora as picking flowers for sale on flower stalls. The source of seeds for our gardens should be seed merchants who *grow their own seed*, or those who retail seed from well-known growers, or carefully selected areas like road verges and derelict airfields, not woods or downs or old meadows or bogs or heaths or dunes or mountains or moors. Needless to say, one should never be tempted to transplant wild plants into one's own garden. Apart from other considerations, this is illegal under The Wildlife and Countryside Act 1981.

Furthermore, one should never broadcast seed of any of the species listed by the Ministry of Agriculture as proscribed weeds – that is to say the spear thistle, creeping thistle, curled dock, broad-leaved dock (which are damaging to crops) and common ragwort (which is poisonous for stock). This does not mean that you cannot grow the ragwort or creeping thistle in your garden, just as we are not forbidden to grow laburnum or lupins or autumn crocus or morning glory. But any plant which has toxic seeds or foliage or which is dangerous to crops, must be rigorously controlled.

There are many botanists who see a great danger in the fairly common practice of importing seeds of wild flowers from the continent. It is obvious that in a perfect world it would be better to keep our flora pure and not contaminate, say, the U.K. strains of oxeye daisies with those from Holland. My own view is that this is inevitable, owing to the fact that the demand for wild-flower seed is at present greater than the local supply. Nor do I think it particularly important. Sir Edward Salisbury pointed out that since the retreat of the ice in Britain, human influence 'must have played an increasingly significant role in the provision of habitats favourable to colonisation of annual species'. Primitive man almost certainly used weed seeds to supplement his grain crops, and no doubt plants from the continent have been introduced by the peripatetic Palaeolithic hunters, the agricultural activities of Neolithic man, by the Iron Age settlers, the Bronze Age farmers and with the cultivated oats (not the wild variety) which were introduced by the Romans. The origins of our weed flora is a good subject for speculation. Turning to the twentieth century: for instance about 22–30,000 acres of lucerne (the seed of which came mainly from abroad) was grown in the eastern counties of the U.K. between 1910 and 1930. This implies, according to Salisbury, that 4680 million foreign weed seeds were sown with the crop during that period. Therefore the introduction of wild flower seed from the continent is nothing new, and should not cause the botanists sleepless nights. Nevertheless, one hopes that growers in this country will rapidly increase their crops of local wild flowers, and preserve our own buttercups and daisies with their particular gene combination. It would be nice to see our farmers growing flowering hay crops as a matter of course, just as we have witnessed them switching to rape as a remunerative break crop for wheat.

At present, however, the art and practice of wild-flower cultivation lies in small gardens, of which school gardens are one of the most important; for if we are to preserve our wild plants and the butterflies which depend on them for survival, they must be ingrained in the minds and hearts of children. To-day only the older members of the public remember – nostalgically – what a field of cowslips looked and smelt like. But we ourselves have no idea how much more beautiful cornfields were in Shakespeare's day – before the advent of drilling and effective seed screening. The now rather scarce purple/red corncockle (*Agrostemma githago*) was a prolific and serious pest of arable crops in the 16th century, and was constantly re-introduced with seed corn. The same is true for the bright golden corn marigold and the cornflower or bluebottle, described by John Clare as 'troubling the cornfields with their destroying beauty'. So modern agricultural efficiency has all but eliminated this once pestilential and beautiful weed. How soon shall we be saying the same about the poppy? It has one advantage over the corncockle whose seed survives only one season, for the poppy's can remain buried yet viable for over a hundred years. At Ashton it flared into a sheet of unexpected scarlet magnificence round the Roman village we had begun excavating. (But poppies are bee, not butterfly flowers.) Incidentally at the bottom of the stone-lined well which we dug out we found, mummified, seeds of the nettle and fat-hen preserved in the mud – probably used as vegetables by the Roman settlers.

Our children, of course, have no idea what their elders and betters are moaning about, and few of us nowadays understand the meaning of Shakespeare's remark: 'The Cockle of rebellion, insolence and sedition which we ourselves have plough'd for, sow'd and scattered . . .' One further generation and it could all be forgotten except in poetry books where 'cockle' and 'cowslip' will be accorded an explanatory footnote.

Within the conventional horticultural-type garden we can also be creative and innovative. In many cases we have accidentally lost the attractive quality of butterfly flowers just as we have bred out 'broodiness' from our hens by concentrating on a big egg output, and rearing chicks in incubators. But there is no reason why we can't reverse the process and produce flowers that will out-buddleia buddleia as butterfly lures. What makes one variety more attractive than another? We simply don't know. Despite the enormous number of books and papers written about butterflies – John Feltwell collected 8000 concerning only the large white – we are singularly ignorant about the *raison d'être* behind butterfly behaviour. Although they feed primarily on floral nectar they are also recorded imbibing fluids from dung, rotting corpses, sap from roots and tree trunks, human perspiration, frog hopper secretions ('cuckoo spit'), aphid honeydew, ripe fruit, wine and urine.

> *Thou dids't drink the stale of horses and the gilded puddle*
> *Which beasts would cough at . . .*

Should we try and incorporate some of these odours in our flower scents? Fortunately we do not have to understand the phenomenon in order to select the crosses and choose the right types of nectar-bearing flowers to experiment with and breed from. We can produce a striped dahlia or a pink daffodil without knowing much about the chemistry of their pigments, and we should be able to breed a super butterfly-flower without understanding a thing about the infinite chemical complexity of plant volatiles.

We are anxious to attract butterflies to the garden because they add to its beauty and charm and interest, but even if these 'flying flowers' do not stay with us to breed, we are doing them a considerable service by providing them with a copious flow of nectar. With the destruction of their habitat and the application of any form of intensive agriculture to their surroundings, they automatically lose the source of their adult sustenance. If butterflies are to survive to breed and locate their now spaced out, far-flung breeding sites, often separated by deserts of flowerless cornfields and burning stubble, they must find nectar *en route*. The day has dawned when the butterfly pub, with its mixture of wild and cultivated flowers, has become an important factor in their conservation. We must also improve the source and quality of garden nectar. I hope we will eventually justify the poets who insist that butterflies love roses. By judicious crossing and some elementary genetics we should be able to add a new category to the growers' catalogues – 'Madam Butterflies' which would be as mysteriously attractive to silver-washed fritillaries as their modest relatives, the brambles.

The Indoor
Butterfly Gardener

CLIVE FARRELL

Introduction

Modern engineering skills have given us such horrors as nuclear reactors, but they have also made large-scale butterfly breeding possible – in a 'silver plastic bubble' where we can create a tropical flower paradise; a warm, sunlit, steamy jungle full of exotic plants, with pools of water, and azure and velvet wings.

David Lowe built, in Guernsey, the first walk-through butterfly house in Europe, and it was he who convinced me that a similar exhibition could and should be set up in London. With much practical help and advice from him I opened the London Butterfly House in 1981. Strolling among the tropical plants and vines or sitting by the pool, the more inquisitive visitor may look beyond the insects on the wing and discover tiny green and yellow eggs, and caterpillars with large frightening eye-spots hiding in the leaves; or a glittering gold and silver chrysalis, suspended from a green twig, or bowls of rotting fruit put out for butterflies to feed from, and perhaps a few tiny quails pecking about in the undergrowth.

All kinds of questions are prompted by such visits: 'How long do butterflies live? Where do they come from? What happens in the winter? Does it cost a fortune to set up? Can we do it for ourselves? What are the quails for?' My aim is to provide most of the answers to these questions.

Surprisingly, perhaps, you do not need to be a millionaire owning a Kew-sized greenhouse – one measuring 8 × 10 feet or a similar sized lean-to conservatory is quite sufficient. Within this structure you must create suitable environmental conditions for your tropical butterflies – warmth, light, humidity and ventilation. Whatever kind of structure you decide upon it must be insect proof, not only to keep in the butterflies, but to keep out their enemies, particularly birds, carnivorous and parasitic native insects. Also it has to contain the correct types of plants for the butterfly species you are breeding: foodplants for the caterpillars and suitable nectar flowers for the

64

adults. When properly set up, you will have created a mini-jungle populated by some of the most beautiful insects in the world.

There are thousands of butterfly species (only a few are British), of which the vast majority are tropical rather than temperate. Their variety is, without exaggeration, quite staggering and their principal habitat is the tropical rainforest. Many are difficult to keep in captivity for, however hard we try, it is virtually impossible to replicate the precise conditions in which they naturally live. The species I have written about are those that are most easily bred, which experience has shown are amenable to the artificial conditions we impose on them, and whose food and nectar plants are not too difficult to cultivate.

The accent in most illustrated books, certainly those aimed at the more popular market, has been on the adult butterflies in all their gorgeous array. However, now that we can breed them, the other stages in their life cycles become just as important and, moreover, have their own intrinsic interest. Any observations on the eggs, chrysalids and caterpillars will more than repay the effort. They will help lessen your failures and possibly be quite new to science – well worth recording for the benefit of other students.

To-day the greatest threat to tropical butterflies is the destruction of their habitat. Adrian Marshall, who investigated the butterfly industry in Taiwan, came to the conclusion that even the fifty million individual butterflies collected each year (1 female to 10,000 males) are not a serious threat to these insects compared to 'the massive habitat destruction and the despoilation of the environment by pollution including pesticides'. Nevertheless those of us engaged in rearing tropical butterflies should never be tempted by rare species but concentrate on those which are still abundant and learn what we can from them. A thorough knowledge of their breeding requirements, their alternative foodplants – in fact every facet of their life style – will help us to battle for their conservation and survival. Perhaps in the not too distant future such information will be required for the re-creation of tropical habitats in nature.

Setting up the Greenhouse

Tropical butterflies are used to higher temperatures than we have in Britain. Although the sun does not reach the recesses of a rainforest, where many of the butterflies live, the ambient temperature is high during the day, seldom less than 70°F throughout the year. At night, however, some tropical species withstand surprisingly low temperatures. In the Cameron Highlands of Malaysia, famous for the size and variety of the insect population, regular night-time temperatures as low as 50°F are recorded. And in Texas, the tropical zebra butterflies *Heliconius charitonius* can even survive freezing, as long as the day temperatures are high enough to thaw them out. A butterfly which remains cold, and therefore inactive, for too long will die of starvation rather than of cold, because without heat these cold-blooded creatures cannot fly. But a word of encouragement here – during that terrible 1981 winter of gales and snow when the electricity failed in my Dorset greenhouse, my colony of postman butterflies *H. melpomene* survived nearly two days of temperatures just above 32°F.

Despite fuel savings, however, such extreme temperatures are not to be recommended for two reasons. Firstly, they will not suit some of the plants you will be using, and secondly, the caterpillars will develop more slowly and will be less able to withstand attacks of viral and bacterial diseases. As temperatures fall, so do their metabolic rates. Minimum night-time temperatures of 55° and day-time temperatures of 72°F are recommended for most tropical butterflies and plants.

There are many greenhouse heating systems, including solid fuel, bottled and town gas, oil, paraffin and electricity. The most expensive systems to install, such as solid fuel, tend to be the cheapest to run and vice versa. Taking all factors into account, electric fan heaters are probably best for our purposes. They are clean, efficient, relatively cheap to purchase and install, and there is the added bonus of warm air movement, beneficial to both the insects and the plants.

Tropical butterflies in the London Butterfly House

They also avoid the danger of incomplete combustion and poisonous fumes inherent with some fuels. Furthermore, during the summer, when excess heat can be a danger, most makes of fan heater can be run cold. It should also be mentioned that an extra radiator run into the greenhouse from a domestic central heating system always helps to provide background heat but is unlikely to be powerful enough on its own to achieve 72°F or more on a cold day.

The power of fan heater you will need will be governed by the cubic capacity of your greenhouse, and advice should be sought from the manufacturer or a heating engineer. They will also need to know the requisite minimum day and night temperatures, and whether, and how, the structure is insulated. I suggest you ask them to read these few paragraphs so that they fully understand the requirements. It is always better to overprovide than to have inadequate heaters. For an average 10 feet × 8 feet greenhouse that is fairly well insulated, two 3 kW heaters with built-in thermostats will be sufficient. You will need two 13-amp power points for the heaters which should be placed on the floor at either end of the structure, and facing each other. One should be set at 72°F and the other at 55°F, the former controlled by a plug-in timer to come on at, say, 9.00 a.m. and go off at, say, 6.00 p.m. Remember that a qualified electrician should always install any wiring system.

Thus you have neatly and simply set up a heating system which will maintain your minimum day and night temperature regimen.

To save up to 40 per cent of the heating costs, the inside of the structure should be lined with thick, clear plastic or, at greater expense, with double-skinned rigid plastic sheets like Correx or Melinex. There are other suitable proprietory systems and most of them include special clips for attaching the material to the glazing bars of the usual aluminium greenhouse. If the structure is wooden, staples or tacks may be used. The butterfly-proof shade netting, described later, insulates the greenhouse further, and also prevents condensation and the resultant drips.

In our latitudes light levels in the greenhouse or conservatory are governed largely by the season of the year, but the siting of structures also plays a part. In midwinter there is only 20 per cent of the midsummer light level. Nevertheless, there are species of tropical butterflies that will survive in our winter-light levels, given sufficient heat, food and nourishment, especially if the greenhouse faces south and is not shaded. Among these are the heliconiid butterflies which in the wild dwell in low light conditions, under the rainforest canopy rather than above. They will visit forest clearings where flowers have sufficient light to bloom, feeding usually from flowering vines of the cucumber family. In my Dorset greenhouse there are no artificial lights but the postman (*Heliconius melpomene*) has survived purely on the tropical plant *Pentas lanceolata* which flowered during the darkest winter periods.

It is difficult to keep the butterflies going over the whole winter. Heating is relatively expensive and, as any horticulturalist will tell you, light levels are as important as temperature, sometimes more so, in getting plants to flower. But if you are determined to try, and you have a north-facing conservatory, the situation is improved by using artificial horticultural lights utilized by growers to induce winter flowering. There are various makes available and again the help of the manufacturers or lighting engineers should be sought. I suggest that a lighting point be situated above the flowering plants, and if possible an automatic timer to extend the day-length in winter.

It is even possible, using such lights, to set up a flight area indoors. It should be emphasized, however, that in the absence of sun or daylight a bank of lights will be required covering the entire ceiling of the flight cage, and this will be rather expensive. The plants will not flower well in these conditions unless placed immediately under the lights and you will have to rely on cut and potted nectar plants and artificial feeders to supplement supplies.

The importance of humidity for the welfare of tropical butterflies and of some of the plants cannot be stressed too much. Many tropical caterpillars are lost through being reared in a dry front room. Chrysalids either fail to hatch or malformed sorry creatures struggle out. Wings of seemingly healthy butterflies quickly become brittle and fray, or eggs fail to hatch. In rainforests, the humidity is often 100 per cent for long periods and rarely drops below 70 per cent – such levels should therefore be maintained in the greenhouse.

Ideally you need an automatic overhead mist spray that comes into operation whenever the humidity falls below 70 per cent. There are various systems on the market suitable for the amateur greenhouse gardener, one of the cheapest automatic systems being controlled by an electronic 'leaf'. In the London Butterfly House and in my Dorset greenhouse the 'rain' is fine enough to mist the atmosphere suffi- ciently but the drops are large enough to roll down the foliage and so water the roots, rather than simply evaporating from the foliage. This dual-purpose method certainly saves time but many gardeners prefer to water their potted plants by hand.

If you are able to attend your greenhouse daily during hot weather an automatic mist spray is not essential. The inside can be damped down by using a hand-held hosepipe with a very fine spray nozzle. Do not worry that fine droplets land on the wings of the butterflies. They soon evaporate or are shaken off with no ill effects. But one word of warning. It does not suit eggs, caterpillars or chrysalids to remain sitting in water for long periods. They prefer to be drip-dry. In fact, a chrysalid is positioned usually hanging under a leaf so that water drops roll off, otherwise the spiracles or breathing holes become clogged up and deadly fungal infections invade.

Conditions of high humidity are also beneficial to most of the plants. Citrus seedlings grow rapidly and dark green, not slowly and with the yellowing leaves so familiar of those raised in dry front rooms. Banana plants grow from seed to 10 feet or more in one season, and *Pentas lanceolata* flowers continuously all year round.

Plants and butterflies do not thrive in a stale, fuggy, static atmosphere. Even in cool conditions fresh air is required and will discourage botrytis and other moulds and fungi which attack plants. In hot sunny weather adequate ventilation is even more important to cool the air and maintain humidity. True, the fan heaters can run cold, and the shade netting and mist spray system all help, but on a very hot day without ventilation the mist spray has to operate full blast to lower the temperature, producing as a result excessive water and increasing the electricity bill unnecessarily.

Automatic ventilation systems include roof vents controlled by cylinders filled with fluids which expand or contract according to the temperature, and electrically operated extractor fans controlled by a thermostat. Whichever system is used, it should be adjusted to open automatically at about 75°F. During a long cold spell the greenhouse should be ventilated manually from time to time to freshen the atmosphere. The air movement from the fan heaters will also help during such periods.

Some juggling with all the automatic controls will be necessary to achieve the right balance. If the heaters are struggling to produce the day-time temperature of 72°F only to cause the vents to open or the mist spray to come into operation and thus lower the temperature, the whole cycle will start again and the net results will be a perpetual cycle of heating and cooling and a large electricity bill!

A small greenhouse set up for tropical butterflies. Among the items shown are: automatic vent and extractor fan; under the roof glass are a horticultural light hanging above the work bench, and a pair of mist spray pipes automatically controlled by a moisture sensor on the capillary matting on the staging; on the floor are two electric fan heaters and a hosepipe; at the far end are the maximum and minimum thermometer, hygrometer and light switch; there are food and nectar plants in the border (which also contains a feeding table), and in pots and jars on the staging, which also supports an emerging cage

We have all seen greenhouses with a summer coat of whitewash or emulsion to prevent tender plants from being scorched. It has usually become grey and streaky as autumn approaches and must be removed in winter to allow maximum light penetration. More elaborate and expensive shading systems involve roller blinds, thermal screens and even automatic slatted blinds controlled by light intensity. We can, however, dispense with all these systems and line the inside of the greenhouse permanently with a simple cheap, cross-laminated polythene netting called Papronet. It has a shading effect of up to 25 per cent in bright sunshine due to its reflective surface but in dull conditions allows up to 94 per cent of light in. In my experience, provided the humidity and ventilation are correctly adjusted, even delicate seedlings are protected from scorching, and in the dead of winter sufficient light penetrates a south-facing structure allowing at least some flower species to bloom. There is also a heat-saving effect of around 20 per cent, and since the material 'breathes', condensation and drips are largely eliminated. In any event, netting is necessary to prevent the butterflies escaping through the vents or windows (if any) and from some from constantly dashing themselves against the glass; it is certainly a bonus that such netting has all the above qualities as well.

The makers of the netting provide special clips for securing it to the glazing bars of a modern greenhouse or, for a wooden structure, battens or staples can be used. It is essential that there are no holes as there is nothing more distressing than butterflies being caught between the glazing and the netting. Also, it is now illegal to release intentionally into the wild any butterfly of a 'kind that is not resident in Britain or is not a regular visitor in a wild state'. Although any escape may be accidental the burden of proof in this respect is on the accused and not the prosecutor. No tropical butterfly, however, would survive a British winter.

If the greenhouse or conservatory is entered from an outside door, a 'lobby' made of netting or at least two over-lapping sheets is necessary to allow you in without being bowled over by a cloud of frantic, flapping butterflies threatening to escape. It is astonishing how butterflies are instantly attracted to a stream of air from outside. Finally, it should be mentioned that even though the mesh of the shade netting is fine enough to keep even the tiniest of butterflies in, and the majority of carnivorous insects out, some of the smaller parasitic flies and wasps which attack eggs, caterpillars and chrysalids will find their way through, as well as some greenhouse pests like whitefly and aphids. However, a finer or more robust netting would be more costly, would impose unacceptably high shading levels, and would impede air flow and efficient ventilation if you were relying on vents rather than an automatic extractor fan. Measures to combat the various enemies which succeed in penetrating your first line of defence can be taken within the greenhouse, using methods discussed later.

Godlike, you now preside over your own space wherein you control the climate. Temperature, light, rainfall, wind and shade are regulated by you, the object being the welfare of your butterflies. These, and their essential companions the plants, are now the missing ingredients.

Nectar and Other Butterfly Foods

We associate butterflies with flowers, and indeed most of our native species as well as the majority of tropical butterflies are nectar-feeders. But food requirements vary depending on the species: some are fairly catholic in their taste, taking other foods as well as nectar, and in fact many prefer rotting, fermenting fruit or bird droppings. An *à la carte* selection includes dung, decaying mushrooms or fungus, decomposing animal remains, honeydew, pollen, sap from wounded trees, mammal urine, mud-puddle cocktail or even human perspiration. Some of these food sources are thought to provide protein and salts to supplement the carbohydrates normally acquired in nectar.

Certain heliconiid butterflies are capable of living for up to eight months assisted by their ability to eat pollen from which they obtain protein, whereas the average exclusively nectar feeding species usually survive only for relatively short periods. The pollen-feeders collect it on specially adapted hairs on the proboscis, later dissolving it in an enzyme and sucking up the resultant soup. In our greenhouse giant owl butterflies can live for three months when on a diet of rotting bananas, and since some swallowtails will feed on fluid oozing from animal remains as well as flowers, perhaps we should supply them with such delicacies, a diet which might prolong their lives in the greenhouse.

Liquid from mud puddles often contains sodium salts but their precise effect on butterflies, sometimes seen feeding in their hundreds, is not yet known. On a recent filming trip in Malaysia, I went to some hot springs where scores of Rajah Brooke's birdwings were feeding, their tongues probing the damp sand. I brought a sample of the water back to England and analysis has revealed that the only significant differences from our average drinking water are high concentrations of sodium and silicates, low chlorine content, and the water was exceptionally soft.

The relative importance of these sodium salts and other substances in providing sustenance essential or desirable for longevity, sexual maturity, sexual stimulation (in both male and female) and in the production and development of eggs has yet to be fully assessed. No doubt controlled laboratory experiments will give us some of the answers in time. Until then the amateur butterfly gardener can only experiment and observe feeding behaviour.

Fresh nectar can be provided in two ways. First, you can cut the right sorts of wild and garden flowers and make them available in vases or jam jars. This is certainly valuable and should be done when nectar from the plants grown in pots or in the greenhouse border seems short – perhaps in the spring, late autumn and winter, but remember that unlike a growing flower, a cut one will cease producing nectar and so has to be replaced every day or two. In spring, sallow catkins are especially valuable and are rich in nectar, as well as pollen for heliconiids. I have seen dozens of these butterflies smothering a sallow branch in a mass of fluttering black and red. Hyacinths, bluebells and scented narcissi are also excellent sources, prepared hyacinths being especially valuable if brought into flower from Christmas onwards. Other suitable plants which flower when our native butterflies are hibernating and so do not normally feed from them, include the various scented viburnums, mahonias, daphnes, *Skimmia* and *Choisya ternata* (the two latter double up as caterpillar foodplants), cinerarias, primulas (especially the winter and spring-flowering *P. malacoides* and *P. obconica*), wallflowers, African violets, jasmine, flowering currants (notably *Ribes sanguineum*) and the winter-flowering honeysuckles *Lonicera fragrantissima* and *L. purpurii*. At least some of the above plants, especially the hardy winter-flowering ones, should be grown in your garden if you intend to keep your butterflies going all year round. Remember that some of the most attractive butterfly plants are heavily scented. Plants which form clusters or masses of small flowers which taper down into a tube, like the buddleias, are particularly suited to the lepidopterous tongue. Some butterfly flowers that seem not to be scented according to the relatively inferior human sense of smell, may be very attractive to insects.

The second and most satisfactory way of providing fresh nectar is through plants growing either permanently in pots or in the greenhouse border if you have one. This is a very important part of indoor butterfly gardening.

The flower structure must be suitable for the butterflies' feeding: *Lantana* is fine but it is useless to offer a butterfly a snapdragon. The flower must also contain nectar. A butterfly may introduce its proboscis into nectarless flowers but, finding the bottle empty, fly off in disgust. If nectar is present it will linger, often nodding its head a few times to probe deeper, and will tend to remain at the same inflorescence to try other flowers. Plants which have long-lasting flowers produced over an extended period are also obvious choices, and although some temperate species thrive in the conditions of tropical warmth and humidity, many do not. Finally, those which only come into flower after growing to an enormous size or after a period of years should be avoided.

No doubt there are many tropical flowers suitable for butterflies, but I can only concentrate on the ones which are obtainable and which have been tried and tested in the London Butterfly House or elsewhere. If you can obtain the appropriate seeds or cuttings you can experiment yourself.

The number one nectar plant for all flower-feeding butterflies is *Lantana camara*, a vigorous tropical shrub in the verbena or vervain family. Although sometimes used as a summer bedding plant in mild districts, it thrives best in a greenhouse with a minimum winter temperature of 40°F, flowers continuously from April to October and will, if permitted, grow 5 or 6 feet tall. The red-flowered variety is a special favourite, notably for swallowtails, its slightly rounded clusters of small tubular flowers having a delicate lemony perfume. Further flowering can be induced by removing the black fruits. It seems to appreciate at least two or three months rest over the winter and in autumn should be pruned to a short stump. It does well in flower pots but even better in a greenhouse border. Seeds may be obtained from specialist seedsmen but it is most easily propagated from cuttings of firm green shoots.

Another plant that does well in pots – but better in a peaty border – is *Pentas lanceolata*. Second only to *Lantana*, this tropical shrub will flower all year round, even in the dead of winter provided the temperature does not fall below 50°F at night and the atmosphere is kept humid. In hot weather it likes to be sprayed daily. Again old flowers should be removed and constant pruning promotes a bushy habit and numerous heads of tubular flowers. There is no discernable perfume, at least to the human nose, but heliconiid and swallowtail butterflies seem to love it. There are, however, a few snags. Very few

Favourite butterfly flowers for the greenhouse. 1 wax flower; 2 *Pentas lanceolata*; 3 *Stephanotis*; 4 *Lantana camara*; 5 heliotrope

British specialist seedsmen list the plant; the seeds are tiny, and the seedlings minute and tricky to handle. But once a plant has been established it is easily propagated from strong green shoots. Plants bear a variety of flower colours from red to pale lilac and white. Being a popular garden plant in southern Africa you may be able to persuade a resident of that part of the world to send you a few seeds in an air mail letter. I obtained my initial stock of seeds from a nurseryman friend in Zimbabwe.

A tropical climbing plant which thrives in humid conditions and needs a minimum winter temperature of about 55°F is the wax flower *Hoya carnosa*. Particularly attractive to danaid butterflies, it will flower three or four times a year, the honey-perfumed, pinkish-white flower umbels literally dripping with nectar. If the roots are kept extra moist while the plant is flowering the blooms will last much longer. This is in the milkweed family and I was fascinated when recently the lesser wood nymph (*Ideopsis gaura*) from Malaysia laid eggs on the young leaves, and two generations reached maturity on the foliage. Before that it had not been recorded as a possible caterpillar food plant for this species, but it was not altogether surprising since it breeds on other plants in the same family.

It is appropriate here to introduce the milkweed genus *Asclepias*. Although its prime use for butterfly breeding is as a caterpillar food-plant for danaid species, including the monarch butterfly (*Danaus plexippus*), the flowers of all species are very attractive to butterflies and at certain times ooze with nectar. The best species for growing in the greenhouse, where it will thrive in the conditions you have created, is the evergreen perennial blood flower *Asclepias curassavica*. It will grow well in pots, and in a greenhouse border will form clumps up to 5 feet tall. It has flat umbels of orange and red flowers, and when broken will bleed the milky-white poisonous sap characteristic of the milkweed family. The greatest care must be taken not to rub this into your eye as the consequences can be very dangerous indeed.

Apart from the tropicals, hardy and half-hardy plants that are very attractive to butterflies are well worth growing permanently in the greenhouse. *Buddleia davidii* grows rather large for the average-sized greenhouse, but if you have the space it is well worth including. It is just as important in the greenhouse as it is outside. Another species *B. fallowiana*, which has light blue, heavily scented flowers and silvery grey foliage is probably an even better bet since it makes a smaller, more manageable bush. The golden-flowered *B. globosa*, if contained in a pot, has the advantage that it flowers early in the year. Again experimentation is desirable.

There are many species of *Hebe* and some will only thrive in cool conditions, but those that will take your greenhouse climate include *H. salicifolia*, 'Great Orme' and 'Midsummer Beauty'. Their advantage over *Buddleia* is a long flowering season and certain species of danaid butterflies, especially the greater wood nymph (*Idea leuconoe*) will sit on a flower spike and methodically plunder every flower. No doubt in this large family of shrubs other species will be found specially suited to tropical conditions.

Inside the greenhouse as well as in the garden heliotrope and marigolds are very popular. *Heliotropium peruvianum* in the greenhouse will grow to 3 or 4 feet and bear panicles of highly scented purple flowers, especially popular with the danaids and nymphalids (including the heliconiids). It is a shrub that will reward you with extra flowers if regularly pruned. It will tolerate relatively shady conditions and, kept warm, will even flower during the winter.

All the daisy family are popular with butterflies and some of the most attractive are the African and French marigolds *Tagetes*. They do, however, resent temperatures higher than about 85°F, tending to grow straggly and etiolated. But with judicious pruning they perk up again in late summer and flower through the autumn. By concentrating on the African marigold *T. erecta*, you will have the bonus that certain exotic swallowtail caterpillars will feed on the foliage.

There are many other plants that, because they will not survive a cold British summer outside, are suitable in varying degrees for the warm greenhouse. Among those worth trying are *Stephanotis*, *Clerodendron*, tender jasmines, various tropical honeysuckles (also useful as foodplants for certain species), *Ixora*, various species of *Eupatorium* – *E. ligustrinum* (*micranthum*) is a useful late autumn-flowering one – and many varieties of single chrysanthemums. Citruses (oranges, lemons, grapefruits, etc.) should also be mentioned here since, although of prime importance for feeding most exotic swallowtail caterpillars, they flower early in the year and have a powerful heady perfume. They can quite easily be grown from a pip, even on a warm windowsill.

At the beginning I dealt with winter and spring-flowering plants suitable as a source of cut flowers to supplement nectar supplies, most of which could be grown outdoors. Other plants, both hardy and half-hardy, that can be grown in pots outdoors and brought in when required include phlox, zinnias (another good pollen source for heliconiids) *Helichrysum* or the so-called 'everlasting' flowers, lilacs, privet, *Sedum spectabile*, Jerusalem artichoke and ornamental thistles, *Centaurea* and various species of *Verbena*. Special mention should be made of *Verbena bonariensis*, which grows quite readily from seed and flowers in profusion from June until October, because it is almost as attractive as *Buddleia* is to native butterflies. Your tropical greenhouse, however, will be too warm for it at the height of summer when it will tend to grow slightly tall and etiolated. I suggest that it is therefore grown in a large pot or container and brought into the greenhouse in late summer which will extend its flowering season, and then left there until the following spring to protect it from frost.

Other plants for pot-growing outside and then introducing when in flower, include most of the cultivated and wild flowers suggested by my co-author. Even a few pots crammed full of flowering dandelions in the spring can be a life-saving elixir of energy for your charges. But remember that the British species of wild flowers and shrubs, and many cultivated species, are adapted to our climate. If left in tropical conditions too long they may become sappy and etiolated and their flowering season shortened. They should be kept in the greenhouse only while flowering and then rejuvenated outside, perhaps to be re-used in the next flowering season.

A nectar-feeding butterfly will almost invariably choose flowers rather than artificial foods – indeed there may be certain substances in natural fresh nectar essential for some function which is not provided in an artificial diet. But there are times when the butterfly population increases dramatically, and the nectar flowers within the flight area are not sufficient to avoid starvation.

One necessary fixture of the greenhouse is a butterfly table. This should be large enough to hold several small dishes and drilled with say a half dozen holes into which short glass or plastic tubes are slotted so that they are flush with the surface. The dishes may contain a selection of rotting fruits: among the favourites are banana, pear, peach, pineapple, plum, apple and orange. In other dishes try some horse or cow manure, rotting prawns or a dead rat or two. All these are successfully used by native butterfly-catchers in Malaysia and other parts of the world as bait in butterfly traps. There are other possibilities based on butterfly preferences in the wild and you will discover other favourites by trial and error.

Opposite, the male *Papilio protenor* touches the female during their courtship flight. Overleaf, flash photograph of a *Euploe core* chrysalis showing jewel-like reflections

The plastic tubes should contain a sugar or honey solution. Experts differ as to the type of sugar to use, whether to use honey at all, and on the strength of the solution. Brian Gardiner has kept successive generations of the large white butterfly for over twenty years, feeding the adults on a 10 per cent solution of ordinary granulated white sugar. He has experimented with other sugars and honey and found no difference in the life span of the adult butterflies. But this is a short-lived species, surviving only two to three weeks. However, some breeders of long-lived butterflies will only use fruit sugar (fructose, usually sold under the brand name Dietade) because it will not crystallize in the butterfly's intestines. Others will only use honey solution, saying that this resembles flower nectar more closely and is therefore more natural. Others will not use honey, claiming it may ferment and thus become harmful. Again, more controlled experiments are required but for safety I suggest that, initially, fructose is used in a 5 to 10 per cent solution – no stronger, as the water will tend to evaporate anyway and the solution may become indigestible. Other tubes could contain maple-syrup solution (which approximates to sap from wounded trees), or salty water for those that need sodium salts. Remember to change and thoroughly clean the tubes at least every 48 hours.

If you are keeping a colony of heliconiid butterflies, one or two of the tubes should contain a small quantity of powdered pollen since this is as essential as nectar to these species. Pollen capsules are usually obtainable in health food stores. These should be opened and the enclosed granulated pollen crushed with the back of a spoon, or you may prefer to reduce the granules to powder in a coffee grinder. The powder, when in an airtight container, seems to keep indefinitely. Although only tiny quantities are needed, larger amounts may be obtained from commercial suppliers, via beekeepers, and one of these is listed in an Appendix.

In laboratory experiments the monarch (*Danaus plexippus*) was able to detect one part of sugar in 200,000! Thus the smell of the food alone will attract them to feed at your butterfly table. For added appeal, however, bright colours in enamel gloss can be painted around some of the feeding tubes to simulate petal shapes. Tropical swallowtails are particularly attracted to bright red flowers but purple, mauve, yellow, orange and white are favoured by a wide range of species. Experiment and observation will tell you which colours are most often visited. As an alternative to paint, pieces of brightly coloured

Opposite, the plain tiger – the commonest butterfly in the world – egg laying in the London Butterfly House. Previous page, wood nymph *Idea leuconoe* drying its wings after emergence

plastic or other waterproof material glued to your butterfly table are just as effective. Some breeders use bird-feeders instead of flat tables, with a collar of brightly coloured material around the feeding bowl; these are as good but I find them more tedious to clean and top up.

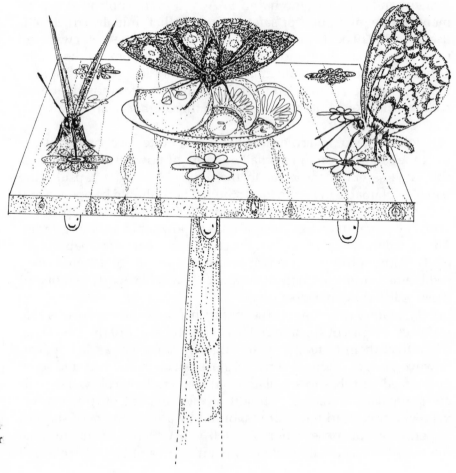

The butterfly table, with fruit and tubes of sugar or honey solution

A Tropical Life Cycle

To see a huge swallowtail hovering over a *Lantana* blossom, fore-wings flapping and hindwings moving slightly to hold the balance, is breathtaking. It is all the more rewarding if you have reared it your-self from the eggs of a previous generation. Since it is beyond the scope of this book to describe numerous species in detail, I will deal with the general breeding principles which apply to many species, but mention only a few. One that is particularly 'easy', even if the flight area is small, is the colourful yellow-and-black swallowtail, the lime butterfly (*Papilio demoleus*) from the Far East.

I will begin with the chrysalis because nearly always it is this stage of the life cycle that is available from dealers and breeders. I suggest you acquire them not earlier than March and not later than October, although most tropicals will breed all year long. Truly tropical species tend to remain in the chrysalis stage for at least two to three weeks, although there are exceptions, while semi-tropical species, including many from Japan and North America, overwinter for up to seven months in this stage. The chysalids, then, are fairly convenient pack-ages for sending through the post. Eggs are also sent but they are apt to dry out and die, while caterpillars need larger containers and foodplants to eat on the way. Also they tend to get knocked about, and overcrowding in a small container may promote diseases.

The package arrives and inside are twelve chrysalids wrapped individually in cotton wool. Carefully unwrap them, removing every strand of cotton wool which otherwise may entangle an emerging butterfly. Several might wriggle quite vigorously and a couple may be darker coloured than the others with yellowish patches discern-able under the wing cases. The latter two are 'colouring-up' to use entomologists' language: that is, they are just about to emerge. They should be taken immediately into the humid atmosphere of the flight area and placed in an emerging cage. The cage should be fully shaded – direct sunlight on the chrysalids can kill them outright or cause

An emerging case

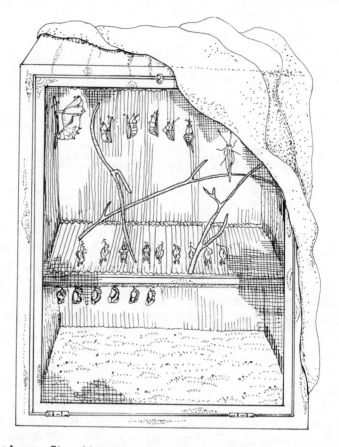

imperfect butterflies. You may think that such a cage is unnecessary but it is quite common for chrysalids, especially those reared in makeshift 'farms' in the tropics, to be affected by parasitic flies or wasps – their worst enemies by far in the wild. In such cases, in place of a beautiful butterfly, numerous nasty buzzing flies emerge from tiny holes in the chrysalis case. These must not be allowed to escape into your flight cage where they may become established and, because they are so small, it is important that the mesh on your emerging cage be extremely fine so that they can be destroyed.

The chrysalids should be carefully laid on a shelf lined with corrugated cardboard. The floor of the cage should have a covering of wet peat or moss to promote extra humidity. (Some breeders spray the chrysalids daily with a fine-mist hand spray but this is not normally necessary if the atmosphere is humid.) The inside of the cage should be rough wood or lined with corrugated cardboard, felt or similar material so that the emerging butterfly can get a grip with the tiny claws on their feet. They need to pull themselves out of the chrysalids and climb up to a suitable position where there is space to allow them to expand and dry their wings. A few rough twigs criss-crossed inside the cage may also help them climb. A newly emerged butterfly is a limp, delicate and vulnerable thing. If unable to get a grip to pull itself out of the chrysalis quickly enough, if it falls or if it is unable to find sufficient space to dry its wings, it will die or at least end up with twisted, malformed wings and be unable to fly. Should this happen, destroy the insect immediately.

The newly emerged butterfly has a swollen distended body and tiny wrapped wings. But the body contains the equivalent of a small 'hydraulic pump' which seems to be triggered on emergence. Once started it does not stop until the correct amount of fluid has been pumped into the wing veins causing the wings to unfold and expand. Eventually they become hard and dry. If the wings are trapped in the pupal case or in some other obstruction during the pumping process a sorry crippled insect results. Wait until the wings are completely dry – at least two hours after full expansion – before you release the butterfly. Of course, any butterfly that starts fluttering before this time has elapsed is ready to leave.

There are other causes that bring about malformed adults or failure to emerge. Both can cause a lot of heartache and it is important to understand what has happened, and so avoid these problems.

The commonest causes of death among chrysalids not collected in the wild (and most of those available in Britain are not) are bacterial, viral or fungal infections. An infected caterpillar is often strong enough to 'make it' to the chrysalis stage only to succumb thereafter. Sometimes even an infected butterfly may emerge and appear perfect but will be debilitated by the infection to the degree that it will refuse to fly at all or collapse and die after a day or two. These difficulties will be dealt with later.

Other causes include poor treatment of the chrysalids; for example, by overheating in full sunlight, or by exposure to low temperatures. Some foreign traders keep them in the refrigerator for too long to delay emergence. Furthermore, if they are stored in a stale wet condition for too long they can be attacked by moulds. Many losses are caused by poor packing. Even a hairline crack in the chrysalis is fatal. Finally, I suspect that a spider or ant bite during the caterpillar stage may be the cause of a dead chrysalis or imperfect butterfly.

Although lime butterflies will emerge successfully from chrysalids simply laid on the corrugated cardboard, in nature they, in common with all swallowtails, all the whites and some of the blues, pupate with the tail anchored to its moorings (usually a twig) and a silk girdle attached further up the mooring, thereby holding the head end at an angle of about 45° to the vertical. If the chrysalids do arrive still attached to twigs simply pin up the twigs inside the cage so that the chrysalis is hanging at the natural angle. If there is no twig you will usually find the remains of the silk anchor pad. Carefully push a pin through this end and into the corrugated cardboard to hold it in position. This is not essential for all species but can help the emerging butterfly to pull itself out of the chrysalis and avoid pulling the case around with it. Nearly all danaids are anchored only at the tail and hang straight down or at a slight angle. Again, pin them through the silk anchor pad, but allow them to hang vertically. If you cannot get sufficient purchase, a tiny dab of contact glue does not harm the chrysalids and will secure them to a cardboard strip which can then be pinned to the bottom edge of the shelf. When the adults emerge, they will turn round on themselves and grip on to the empty pupal case and dry their wings there.

At some stage during emergence and wing drying the butterflies excrete the residue of waste fluid (mecomium) produced as a by-product of the change from caterpillar to butterfly. It is a rather toxic fluid and in quantity could adversely affect fresh chrysalids or butter-flies if they can sit around in it. The cardboard and the peat at the bottom of the emerging cage therefore need renewing at regular intervals, and it is a good idea to give the cage a good wash with mild disinfectant from time to time.

Anyway, to return to the lime butterflies themselves, the first two emerge in quick succession the following morning. Tropical butter-flies almost invariably hatch in the morning rather than the afternoon – we don't know why. On release into the flight area they fly up against the netting a few times. One sips droplets of water from the netting; the other dips and dives around the various flowers then hovers over a *Lantana* blossom and feeds. Soon they are both feeding avidly, particularly on some sprays of *Buddleia* put in a vase for them. Occasionally they circle around and hover above each other with antennae waving, but they are both males.

Two days later three more insects emerge, and later that day, in an intense courtship display, one male hovers above a female and appears to be fanning her with his wings. Judging by Unno's photo-

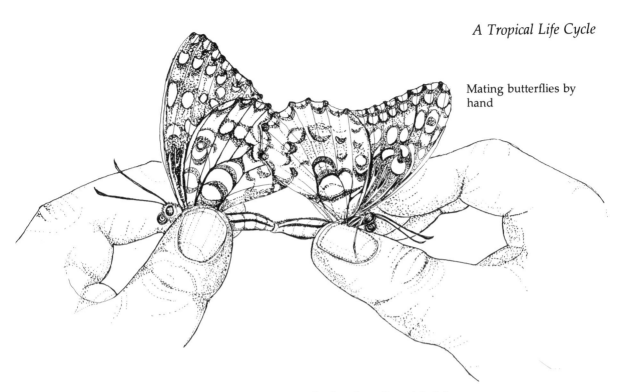

Mating butterflies by hand

graph of *P. protenor* the male appears to touch the female with his tongue. Mating occurs shortly afterwards and they remain joined for three hours. The length of time during which this occurs varies and in butterflies is certainly not a momentary affair, some pairs occasionally remaining in this position overnight.

As the male introduces the spermatophore or sperm sac into the female, his abdomen pumps gently. When she later lays her eggs each one will be fertilized individually as it passes by the spermatophore, its contents being adequate to fertilize all her eggs.

Although my aim has always been to create natural conditions in which mating occurs spontaneously, some breeders find it an advantage at times to mate butterflies by hand. Not all species respond to this technique but swallowtails seem to be especially amenable. Before you start make sure that both partners are well fed, at least a day old and thoroughly warm.

The female and male are then gently held in each hand at the base of their wings and abdomens. Your index finger and thumb should apply slight pressure to the male's abdomen causing the claspers at the tip of his abdomen to open, exposing the male organ between. You should also apply pressure to the female's abdomen causing her to reveal her sex organ as well. Then fit the male claspers carefully around the female's abdomen and slowly relax the pressure on the male so that a bond is formed. Keep the female uppermost and, when they are joined, place the female on the netting with the male hanging down beneath her. If you fail to achieve a union after a couple of attempts, leave them alone and try again later. It is quite a difficult operation and you may need an expert to demonstrate the technique before you are able to master it.

A day or so after separation from the male, the female flies off and appears to ignore flowers. Instead she investigates certain green leaves and shoots, occasionally hovering about them and 'drumming' on them with her forelegs. She takes particular interest in a small potted Mexican orange bush (*Choisya*) and suddenly curls her body round and, still hovering, deposits a tiny greenish-yellow egg.

Life over the next two weeks or so is a pattern of feeding, egg-laying and displays to amorous males designed to tell them she has already mated. Over this period she will have laid 75 or more eggs. Finally, her wings and those of her companions become frayed and torn and fifteen days from emergence you will find her dead on the floor. She has lived her allotted span, much longer than the average for her species in the wild.

Meanwhile, caterpillars from her eggs and from others are hatching. Tiny dirty-white-and-black caterpillars that bear an uncanny resemblance to bird droppings, appear on top of the leaves of the Mexican orange bush.

We must pause here to consider one of the greatest difficulties facing the amateur indoor butterfly breeder, that of growing or acquiring the right caterpillar foodplants in sufficient quantities.

I'll deal with the foodplants themselves first. The tropical butterfly chart (see Appendix) clearly shows that caterpillars are very exacting in their requirements. Certain butterfly families tend to favour specific plant families, and some would sooner die than eat the wrong foodplant. Since the life history of the overwhelming majority of the world's butterflies is unknown, one can sometimes only make an educated guess at the foodplant for a species based on the preferences of other members of the same family. Here the amateur butterfly gardener has a real contribution to make to science – substitute foodplants for many species being discovered in a process of trial and error or by sheer accident. For example, the beautiful Paris peacock (*Papilio paris*) was thought to favour only plants in the Rutaceae family. In the London Butterfly House they laid on willow and sallow, representatives of an entirely different family, and the caterpillars fed up on the foliage and produced perfect adults. Although such surprises occur, with caterpillars taking plants quite unrelated botanically to their normal fare, they are very much the exception. Experience usually suggests that in the absence of the normal foodplant it is worth trying a butterfly on related ones (that is to say, plants in the same family), but, even so, there are many instances where the females will refuse to lay or the caterpillars to eat, and where the substitute may even kill them. If, for example, a European large white eats wallflower, the caterpillar dies in its first instar and, similarly, the monarch larva dies if it eats oleander.

Because of the quantities required, it is essential to grow the foodplants either in pots or, if they are hardy, in the garden. Alternatively you need to have access elsewhere to adequate supplies of growing plants – perhaps from a park or recreation ground or even from a derelict site. I know of some enormous bushes of *Skimmia japonica* growing in the gardens of some houses scheduled for demolition for a motorway scheme. These bushes have sustained several hundred of my exotic swallowtail larvae over the past two years, likewise a friend's Amur cork tree, a hardy deciduous ash-like tree from northern China that has grown within the space of three years to over 30 feet high. Both plants belong to the Rutaceae family, and are therefore related to the *Citrus* species which are the chosen foodplants of tropical swallowtails in the wild.

Many species of tropical butterfly foodplant are also very attractive garden plants as well. The common garden shrubs, Mexican orange and *Skimmia japonica*, have dark green shiny leaves, and fragrant white flowers in the spring and sometimes again in the autumn. The female and hermaphrodite plants of the *Skimmia* also have bright red berries which last through winter. Rue, the garden herb from which the family takes its name, forms a small round bush, the foliage of which has a pleasant orangey perfume when lightly bruised between the fingers. Incidentally, all three can easily be grown from cuttings rooted over winter in a peat/sand mixture.

Other important caterpillar foodplants which will survive our winter and grace the shrubbery and herbaceous border, or the front porch, include various milkweeds, bamboos, passion flower vine, buckthorn, sallow and willow, honeysuckle, false acacia and Dutchman's pipe *Aristolochia durior* (just about hardy in mild districts); others are listed in an Appendix.

Many good foodplants are not hardy outside but can be grown in the greenhouse, conservatory or, in some cases, the front room. Some of them make most attractive house plants. One foodplant worth mentioning is oleander, a plant with deliciously almond-scented flowers and a foliage which feeds several of the danaids. It is a good plant for the dryish conservatory, and will withstand zero temperatures as long as it is not wet. Others are the perennial ever-green blood flower *Asclepias curassavica*, essential if you are breeding milkweed-feeding species during the winter or early spring; banana (some species, including the Abyssimian banana, can even be treated as summer bedding plants); the popular houseplant *Ficus benjamina*; paw-paw and custard apple (both easily grown from pips and obtainable from fruiterers specializing in exotic fare); all species of *Citrus* including lemon, lime, orange and grapefruit (all also grown easily from pips); sweet potato (simply bury the corms and keep them warm) and *Cassia*. The richly scented climbing vines, wax flower and *Stephanotis*, are in the milkweed family and will double up as food-plants for certain species of nymph butterfly as mentioned in the previous chapter. People with children should remember that the seeds of oleander, *Asclepias* and *Cassia* are toxic.

Returning once again to the lime butterfly caterpillars, let us assume there are half a dozen Mexican orange bushes in pots, a small clump of rue in the garden, a couple of lemon seedlings on the kitchen windowsill and access to a large *Skimmia* bush in a friend's garden four miles away. Your dozen butterflies included four females all of which mated and there are now about 40 caterpillars and over 200 eggs. Growing caterpillars, especially those of large swallowtails, consume prodigious quantities of foliage. If all 200 eggs were allowed to develop, all these stocks of rutaceous plants would be devoured, and you would probably leave your friend's *Skimmia* a small and sorry looking stump. If all the caterpillars were to pupate and in due course produce commensurate numbers of offspring the foodplant problem would become quite desperate.

Unless you have enormous stocks of the right foodplants, and almost unlimited space and time, there is only one answer – birth control. In the wild only an average of two butterflies will emerge and survive per hundred eggs but in captivity, because of the near ideal conditions and lack of predators – if you've set your greenhouse up correctly – considerably more are capable of surviving. If you over-crowd the caterpillars, suitable leaves will be more difficult for them to find and they will expend energy marching all over the place looking for them, and will come into contact with each other much more than necessary, with the effect of promoting and spreading contagious diseases. Some species will even turn cannibalistic.

It is best to decide in advance how many caterpillars the available stocks of foodplant will sustain, taking into account the stock requirement for future generations or other species, and destroy the surplus eggs. I find it far easier to crush an egg than kill a caterpillar – let alone a healthy butterfly before it has lived a reasonable life. The importance of such methods of control cannot be over-emphasized. You will end up with fewer but healthier butterflies. If you can judge foliage consumption to a degree that there are at least a few leaves left on the potted plants, you will find they will recover better than those which have been totally defoliated. In fact the latter will often die. You may decide, for example, you have sufficient foliage for 40 caterpillars; you could pass on 50 eggs to a fellow enthusiast and crush the rest.

By far the best way of rearing caterpillars is on healthy foodplants in pots. Distribute them among your *Choisya* bushes which should be sleeved with a very fine netted material to stop them getting out and to prevent their predatory enemies, the ants, spiders and parasitic flies from getting in, and simply left. I use crystal clear plastic film densely punctured with tiny holes – the same material that is often used in supermarkets to package bread. Its advantages are that you can clearly see what is going on inside, and the holes are sufficiently adequate to provide ventilation yet small enough to exclude even the tiniest parasite. Stand the pot on capillary matting so it is watered by capillary action. The baby caterpillars should only be touched, and then gently and carefully, with a tiny soft brush. They should never be moved when about to change their skins – or their silk anchor pad will be damaged so that when the old skin splits they will not be able to ease themselves out of it. This invariably kills them. The frass (caterpillar droppings) will fall onto the soil in which the plant is growing. If there seems to be an undue build up, or if any mould starts forming on the frass it should be removed.

If supplies of potted foodplant are limited or if you wish to conserve it for the future, the caterpillars can be transferred to cut foodplants. Remember that newly hatched caterpillars favour young leaves or shoots, although there are exceptions. Some species will swap species of foodplant quite happily – others would sooner starve. The lime caterpillars will happily transfer to *Skimmia*. Place the stems of the *Skimmia* cuttings in a water bottle, being careful to plug the neck of the bottle around the stems with paper or cotton wool. Most caterpillars have an insane desire to walk down into the water and drown.

If the caterpillars are larger you may well find that they grip so hard with their suction pad-like feet that they cannot be moved with the brush. In this case cut off the twigs or leaves where they are resting with a pair of secateurs, and simply pin or tie the twigs and leaves to the cut foodplant. The cuttings can either be sleeved in the same way as potted foodplants, or placed inside a small cage. The cage can be made of wood, plastic, or other materials as long as at least one side is covered in mesh to allow ventilation. Just like the sleeves, it should be spider and ant proof. Whether the caterpillars are sleeved or caged, their frass should be removed daily to avoid diseases. The bottom of the cage can be lined with kitchen paper or tissue, which can simply be thrown away.

The cut foodplant will have to be changed at least every three days or when an obvious shortage becomes apparent, whichever is the sooner. It is vital that the leaves are fresh.

Rearing hundreds of caterpillars on cut foodplants is a very labour-intensive occupation. Force yourself to cut the numbers down. Each butterfly is equally beautiful and will thrive much better with adequate nectar supplies. There is more merit in careful observation of each stage, perhaps of an unusual species, supported with notes and photographs, than in rearing record numbers.

Another method of rearing caterpillars, more appropriate for small species with smaller appetites, involves keeping them with their foodplant in airtight containers, the floor and sides lined with absorbent tissue. This is even more labour intensive since the food needs changing every day. Although in an airtight container leaves keep relatively fresh, the static atmosphere within tends to encourage moulds and fungi. The box must, therefore, be cleaned out every day and relined with fresh tissue. First, above the old leaves, put fresh ones on which the caterpillars will crawl. The next day, the old leaves should be removed after checking for caterpillars that have lagged behind – perhaps changing their skins – and a further layer of new leaves added. Under no circumstances should such containers be stood in direct sunlight – or directly on top of a radiator. The contents will heat up and die very quickly.

Our star caterpillars have lost their bird-dropping disguise and now possess frightening false-eye markings on their heads – evolved to scare predators that could no longer be deceived by over-large bird droppings. They also possess in common with all swallowtail larvae unique glands, positioned between the false eyes and the head, called osmateria. These are two fleshy orange-coloured horns which shoot out when the animal is disturbed and emit a very pungent citrus odour thought to be a defence against ants, spiders and possibly other predators.

At a constant 72°F, the lime butterfly can develop from baby caterpillars to chrysalids in as little as 14 days. When ready to pupate, they anchor their tails, loop round their silk girdles and, apart from the occasional spasm, remain quiescent. In this condition they are very delicate and should not be touched. They appear to shrivel and shrink, and with a final wriggle, the skin splits and rolls off leaving a brand new chrysalis underneath. This is very soft at first and should not be touched for at least two days.

Ideally the chrysalis should be left attached to its moorings. This may involve snipping off a twig or, if it is on the sleeve, this can be turned inside out. If it is dispensable and there are several chrysalids on it, cut into appropriate pieces. If the chrysalis has to be removed, perhaps to send off to a fellow member of an entomological society, carefully cut through the silk waist girdle and with the point of a pin ease away the silk anchor pad from its moorings. On no account pull it off – a crippled or dead butterfly will result.

The cages should now be cleaned and they and the plant sleeves disinfected. (Indeed, the greenhouse itself must be kept clean at all times.) I use crystal-clear cellophane netting sleeves, which I throw away after use, thereby avoiding further problems.

You have now gone full circle. Although there are differences in caterpillar behaviour and eating habits, the above will serve as a useful model for most species.

More Butterflies
for your Greenhouse

At the London Butterfly House in the height of summer there may be as many as fifty different species on the wing. Of course, the flight area is enormous with corresponding quantities of nectar plants and caterpillar foodplants. There is also a wide range of microclimates there: the north side tends to be cooler than the south; the temperature at ground level can be as much as 10°F cooler than that at the ceiling; some areas remain damper and therefore cooler than others; and there are some very wet areas at the pools' margins.

The butterflies are free to choose the conditions that suit them best. Native brimstones and peacocks, which require temperate conditions, live alongside plain tigers (*Danaus chrysippus*) which can take relatively hot dry conditions; and heliconiids, Paris peacocks (*Papilio paris*), red helens (*P. helenus*), common mormons (*P. polytes*) and owl butterflies (*Caligo*), all of which thrive in warm to hot humid conditions. I must emphasize that the range of species you can keep is governed by the size of your greenhouse and the conditions you maintain within it. The chart in Appendix 2 gives you further guidance.

From my own experience, albeit in a large area, some of our more powerful native butterflies happily co-habit with their exotic cousins provided the temperature does not regularly exceed 90°F. These include the painted lady, peacock, small tortoiseshell, red admiral, comma, wall brown, speckled wood, large and green-veined whites, clouded yellow and brimstone. But on a hot summer's day, even with the vents fully open and the boiler fan running cold, the temperature rises into the nineties and it certainly becomes too hot for many temperate species. These rest near the soil, fanning and vibrating their wings to cool themselves until late afternoon when with the drop in temperature they take off again.

Temperate species from southern Europe, where the summers are longer and hotter, have done very well. The southern white admiral produced several generations and overwintered on a honeysuckle bush, and the somewhat brighter and smaller continental speckled wood laid its eggs, and fed the caterpillars quite happily on bamboo!

It is worth looking at some of the tropical species that have been tried and tested in small greenhouses in more detail.

Two species that lend themselves especially well as residents of the indoor butterfly garden are the postman (*Heliconius melpomene*) and its close relative the zebra (*H. charitonius*). Although the rearing methods mentioned in the previous chapter will work well for these species, there is another method that involves very little work and should create regular supplies of butterflies over many months. Roy Stockley, who has a lifetime's experience of breeding butterflies, suggested that I grow their foodplant, *Passiflora caerulea*, in hanging pots suspended by wires from the greenhouse roof. Although unsleeved, ants would be prevented from finding their way into the foliage and carrying off eggs or young caterpillars. Spider predation would also be considerably reduced. In fact, I found that the butterflies' eggs, laid on the tendril tips or young leaves, hatched and developed into adults with little attention. Of course, a few were lost to spiders but these losses were easily sustained due to the large number of eggs laid. However, the *Passiflora* did not enjoy growing in the suspended pots with its vines hanging down rather than climbing up, and it resented being positioned in full sunlight during the summer. So, I removed them every few weeks to stand in a shady place, with some canes to climb up and they soon recovered. Heliconiid butterflies are capable of living for several months in perfect conditions and it is an abiding joy to see a strong colony of them hovering among the flowers. It is even possible after a while to recognize individuals by particular tears in their wings or by their relative sizes.

One of the easiest tropical swallowtails to breed is the common mormon (*Papilio polytes*). This large black-and-yellow insect is common in the Oriental regions, nearly always available from British dealers, and is frequently exchanged between amateur entomologists. Interestingly there are two female forms. The usual female markings are similar to those of the male, while the other form closely resembles a quite different swallowtail, *Pachliopta hector*. The latter, as a caterpillar, feeds on poisonous *Aristolochia* vines and sequesters the acid from the plant which probably protects it from many would-be predators. By copying or mimicking her markings the female common mormon tricks her predators into thinking she is equally poisonous, thus increasing her chances of survival. This is an example of Batesian mimicry which is not uncommon in butterflies. It is quite probable you will breed both female forms in varying proportions.

This species will mate in relatively confined conditions and will fly at low light levels. Norwood Hall Horticultural College in Middlesex has set up a small flight area (18 feet long × 9 feet deep) by sectioning off part of a lean-to greenhouse. During the first year of operation the college succeeded in producing several hundred of this species. The eggs were laid on potted rue plants on which the baby caterpillars started to feed. They were then transferred to *Skimmia japonica* foliage kept in water bottles in a cage. At the end of September, when the flight area was closed for the winter, I was presented with over 300 healthy chrysalids!

Other suitable swallowtails for the smaller greenhouse include the dark mormon (*Papilio protenor*) and the Christmas butterfly (*P. demodocus*) both of which usually feed only on plants of the rue family but sometimes they will feed on the African marigold and cosmos. It is thought that these plants contain essential oils and aromatic substances which have some similarity to those contained in their usual rutaceous foodplants. Indeed, if you crush the leaves their aroma resembles that of Mexican orange or citrus leaves. I should warn you, however, that although I have reared both these species quite successfully on marigold (African *not* French) other enthusiasts have had poor results – the caterpillars dying in the second or third instar. More research is required but I would guess that other swallowtail species may be persuaded to feed on it.

The orange dog (*P. anchisiades*) is common in South America and parts of the West Indies. Chrysalids are regularly sent to me by Clive Urich, who has had a lifetime's experience of breeding butterflies in the rainforests of Trinidad. It takes to Mexican orange quite happily and is unusual in that the female lays eggs in batches rather than singly, and the caterpillars feed gregariously.

Other swallowtails likely to be available include species which utilize various species of *Aristolochia* as caterpillar foodplants. Most of them will take to Dutchman's pipe which is just about hardy in mild districts. They will also feed on our the birthwort (*A. clematitis*), which is a hardy deciduous herbaceous plant with fresh-looking

The zebra butterfly *Heliconius charitonius* – a Neotropical species – on its foodplant *Passiflora caerulea*

apple green, distinctly veined leaves that has become naturalized in some parts of Britain.

The common rose (*Pachliopta aristoclochiae*), a tropical swallowtail from the Oriental region, is one of the easiest to breed. It is predominantly black and has vivid red markings and long tails. It stores aristolochic acid sequested by the larva from its foodplant – various species of *Aristolochia* – and serves as a model for other swallowtails in nature which are not themselves poisonous. A vine they favour, *A. tagala*, often grows over 200 feet tall. With luck, seeds can be obtained and once germinated the seedlings are very vigorous. They require high humidity and a minimum temperature of 50°F.

Among the sulphurs and the whites, two interesting species are often available here, the African migrant (*Catopsilia florella*) and the great orange tip (*Hebomoia glaucippe*). The former resembles a large, pale, clouded yellow. The latter is a giant version of our own native orange tip and its caterpillars are fascinating creatures with false eye markings and bright red and blue hoops around the prolegs. They will rear up like snakes when disturbed. They take readily to the spider flower *Cleome spinosa*, a beautiful old-fashioned half-hardy bedding plant. It is well-worth planting out in the garden during the frost-free months and grows into a tall spiny plant having variable white, pink and cyclamen-coloured flowers, and a strange, strong mustard-oil aroma. You will find that small and green-veined whites will lay happily on it and in captivity it is eagerly devoured by the large white's caterpillar. It is easily grown from seeds sown in pans under cover in early spring. The caterpillar of the great orange tip will also feed on plants in the closely related cabbage family including cabbage itself, Brussels sprout leaves, rape and wall-rockets. No doubt other plants that contain mustard oils would also be taken although *Cleome* is preferred for laying on. It can also be reared on artificial diet.

The danaid family, including the tigers, crows and nymph butterflies, occurs chiefly in the Far East, India, Australia, and Africa. They are tough, long lived nectar-feeding insects, although some species will take liquid from rotting carrion, manure and damp mud. One of the toughest and best known species is the monarch (*Danaus plexippus*), which rapes rather than courts its female, and is an inhabitant of North America. In the winter this butterfly migrates south to Mexico, where millions congregate in certain parts of the forest and hibernate in large dense clusters. The monarch is a great traveller and occasionally crosses the Atlantic to reach Eire and southwest England. It has colonized New Zealand within the last 100 years, and at some period established itself in Australia and the Canary Isles. The caterpillars sequester and store heart poisons (akin to digitalis, used in human medicine) from their food plant, which are then passed on via the pupa to the adults and eggs to protect them from their many potential predators.

The great majority of danaids feed on milkweeds and the related Apocynaceae, many species of which contain heart poisons. As we have seen (p.40) once the butterfly has emerged from the chrysalis it actively seeks other chemicals (pyrrolizidine alkaloids) from both wilting plants foliage and certain nectars. It requires these, both for protection from predators, especially spiders, and for the manufacture of sex attractants. In order to stimulate their sexual drive it is useful to provide bunches of the appropriate wilting foliage – for instance bunches of groundsel or heliotrope – which can be suspended in the greenhouse and from which the butterflies can imbibe the alkaloid-laden juices. Species like the common crow (*Euploea core*), the blue-striped crow (*E. mulciber*), the lesser wood nymph (*Ideopsis gaura*) and the plain tiger (*Danaus chrysippus*) can be seen crowding on these dying bunches of leaves and stems. The latter species is so 'hooked' on these chemicals, that in the wild it even sucks the juices from the bodies of dying grasshoppers which have been feeding on the appropriate plants. Danaids can, of course, only take fluid food, and sometimes they follow other insects with biting mouthparts which chew up leaves, and harvest some of the sap oozing from damaged foliage.

The monarch is likely to be one of the first species available to the indoor butterfly gardener because it mates easily and sometimes lays over 100 eggs. The caterpillars, if kept warm and humid enough, grow at a prodigious rate and are capable of going from egg to chrysalis within two weeks. They are quite charming creatures in their black and orange hooped livery with waving black tentacles. Make sure you have sufficient foodplants for they are the Billy Bunters of the lepidopterous world! Almost all species of milkweed are suitable as foodplants. The blood flower *Asclepias curassavica*, mentioned in a previous chapter as a nectar plant, can be propagated from seeds sown in pans in the greenhouse or by lifting and dividing established plants. *A. syriaca* (which can be grown outside in the garden) and *A. rubra* are so tough you can even cut the roots into pieces and when replanted a new plant will sprout from each. *A. curassavica* cannot survive temperatures below 50°F.

In the same family as our browns is the massive giant owl (*Caligo memnon*) from Brazil. This and other large *Caligo* species are powerful insects that have realistic eye markings on the underside of the lower hind wings. When disturbed the giant owl will flash its wings and present a frightening owl 'face'. This defence mechanism is calculated to deter foraging birds, mammals and lizards. The top surface of the wings has a dark blue, slightly metallic sheen. In other species of *Caligo* the blue is much brighter and lighter and quite beautiful. The butterflies will feed on a variety of rotting, even fermenting fruit. They sometimes gorge themselves for an hour or more and, on occasions, become quite inebriated, flopping over on their sides and remaining so until the effects have worn off! This species needs space to fly and is unsuitable except for the larger greenhouse or conservatory. If you can accommodate it, however, it is easy to feed and is long lived. It lays rounded white eggs in batches both on top and underneath banana leaves. The eggs turn orange unless they are infertile. The caterpillars deserve a special mention. In my greenhouse at the time of writing, I have a fully grown one, which measures $5\frac{1}{2}$ inches long and $\frac{1}{2}$ inch wide at the broadest place. It has eight horns on its head, four spikes along its back and a forked tail.

Banana plants can quite easily be grown from seed, which is available for several species, one of the hardiest being the Abyssinian banana *Musa ensete*. This particular species will even succeed as a summer bedding plant in warm districts. The seeds of all should be soaked for a day before sowing in a peaty compost. They grow at an incredible speed and it is quite possible to obtain a plant 6 feet or more tall from a spring sowing. The appetite of the owl caterpillars is such that you will need all the foliage you can obtain. If a plant becomes impossibly large for the space available, prune it down, and in time a fresh shoot will appear from its base. The old plant can then be cut away at the root and the new one will take over. There is a miniature banana *Musa coccinea* which, growing to only 4 feet, is more suitable for indoor culture or for a small greenhouse.

Caterpillar, chrysalis and adult of the common crow *Euploea core* on an oleander – one of its foodplants

Owl butterflies have also been known to utilize related plants, including the beautiful bird of paradise flower *Strelitzia reginae*, as well as various species of coarse grasses, bamboos and even lilies. It is worth experimenting with other monocotyledons. I have known owl butterflies pass through a British winter as caterpillars – feeding

sporadically on warm days and completing their development in the spring. However, do not expose them to temperatures below 50°F.

Distantly related to the peacocks and tortoiseshells of the large Nymphalidae family is the widespread diadem butterfly (*Hypolimnas misippus*), which is found throughout the warmer parts of the world. The adult is long lived and prefers rotting fruit to flowers. The female, like one of the female forms of the common mormon, also exhibits Batesian or modified Mullerian mimicry. She is quite different from the male in her colour and marking, strongly resembling the poisonous plain tiger, while he is purple with whitish patches on fore and hind wings. So different are the sexes that visitors to my butterfly house often refuse to believe they are the same species. It was thought that the female of the diadem was avoided by predators because of her similarity to the poisonous plain tiger, but it is now known that she too is rather toxic, so the two butterflies probably enjoy mutual benefits from the resemblance. In captivity the diadem's caterpillars can be reared on stinging nettles.

Breeding Native Butterflies

In the chapter entitled 'Will Butterflies Stay?' my co-author has suggested that you might persuade certain native species to stay and breed in your garden by confining them at first in a large enclosure. You may, however, wish to go further and rear them in breeding pots for releasing either into your flight cage or into your garden. I have already mentioned the species which will breed in the greenhouse, but because our British natives are adapted to our cold temperate climate most will only thrive outdoors. I must again stress that it is pointless to release captive-bred butterflies which have no hope of survival.

There is considerable controversy among 'experts' on the subject of the release of bred butterflies into the wild. As in all reasoned arguments there are 'pros' and 'cons', but without going too deeply into the matter, my opinions can be quite simply expressed. Whichever species you breed, never release a rare butterfly, like a purple emperor or swallowtail, into the wild for this could conceivably infect a fragile wild colony with a cage-induced disease. For the same reason do not try to 'top-up' a small colony of sedentary wild butterflies with captive-bred ones. However, if the species is a wide-ranging or migratory insect, any disease which may have developed in your breeding cage will have little chance of spreading due to relatively sporadic contact with wild individuals. An introduction of a sedentary common butterfly, like the small copper, into a newly created and seemingly suitable habitat where they do not already occur would in my opinion be justified. All the same, such attempted introductions must be made under the auspices of the Nature Conservancy Council or one of the local natural history societies approved by it.

Lack of space precludes me dealing in depth with each species but certain general principles apply to all. The netted fruit cage will certainly keep out enemies like birds, mice and even inquisitive cats, but within this more control can be exercised by confining pairs of butterflies in netted flowerpots, – a method Derek Arthurs has used successfully for many years. A 12–15 inch flowerpot containing the growing foodplant is sleeved in a dome-shaped fine black nylon net about 18 inches high, which is supported by a frame made from three or four hoops of wire tied at the apex. A generous pad of cotton wool soaked in a 5 per cent honey- or sugar-water solution is placed on top of the dome and resoaked daily. Because caged butterflies tend to gravitate upwards they inevitably come into contact with the feeding pad. Most common species will feed quite happily on this for several weeks, but remember that butterflies do need sunshine for at least part of the day or they will not mate (although exceptions occur). On no account over-expose the breeding pot and its inhabitants to direct sun on a hot summer's day.

While wild-caught paired females of the majority of native species will usually lay their remaining eggs quite happily in the net-covered flowerpot, freshly emerged bred butterflies must be persuaded to mate before fertile eggs can be obtained. If pairings fail to take place in the netted flowerpot it may be because the butterflies have inadequate space. It would then be worth trying a somewhat larger cage, say about 3 feet square and high.

The requirements necessary for successful butterfly pairings in captivity are difficult to define precisely and some failures can be expected. However, provided the following basic conditions can be produced the success rate for most common species is high.

1. Warmth and protection from wind. In spring and early summer the temperature should be higher than that outside – say 70° to 75°F – because the captive butterflies, unlike those in the wild, may not be able to fly to a warm spot.
2. Sunshine. This is difficult to order, but for most species is essential (speckled woods should be happy in dappled shade), although it is surprising how many species will pair on dull days provided they are warm enough. On such days, moving the butterflies into a warm greenhouse may very well induce pairings.

When these conditions have been satisfied, introduce the freshly emerged butterflies into the netted flowerpot or cage – but on no account overcrowd. Males will usually be the first to emerge from a batch of chrysalids and once they are feeding well and used to their surroundings, introduce the fresh females. This is best done while

A flowerpot adapted for use as a miniature breeding cage

they are expanding their wings, and pairing may very well occur within a few minutes.

Sometimes, butterflies resulting from common parents will refuse to mate despite apparently optimum conditions. Try introducing one or a few wild insects of the same species and immediate pairings are often secured.

Much experience can be gained by observation. For example, many butterflies, having been inactive during a dull morning will readily pair during a sudden bright spell of sunshine. In difficult cases, keeping the insects in the dark for 24 hours and then releasing them into the light often does the trick.

Among the advantages of using these relatively small enclosures are first, the butterflies are induced to come into regular contact with each other, thereby greatly increasing the chances of their mating; second, once mated, the female is in continuous contact with the caterpillar foodplant, which stimulates her to lay eggs.

In order to obtain the maximum number of eggs from the freshly mated females, it is essential that sufficient quantities of foodplant should have been organized in advance – ideally there should be enough to take the caterpillars through to the chrysalis stage. Incidentally, some species, despite the presence of foodplants, may lay their eggs on the netting or side of the pot.

While most native butterflies need sunshine to encourage mating, it is not so essential for caterpillars, and many chrysalids will die if exposed to direct sun. Those of silver-washed and marsh fritillaries are particularly vulnerable.

Native butterflies which hibernate as adults should be placed in a cold spot well protected from earwigs, spiders, and other enemies by tough netting. Do not try to mollycoddle them by keeping them in a warm room, or they will perish. But they do need airy conditions to avoid contracting fungal diseases. On a warm spring day place them in the sun and hand feed them with honey or sugar water if they will not feed naturally. Remember that the autumn brood of small tortoiseshells, commas and peacocks do not become sexually mature and therefore will not mate unless they have hibernated.

The cultivation of various foodplants is dealt with in an Appendix, so I need add nothing here, except that for our particular purposes I recommend you use sterilized loam rather than garden soil. Since its nutrient content is higher, the plants become more lush and at the same time you will avoid the plant and insect pests present in ordinary soil. To keep the latter even further at bay, always cover the flower pot drainage holes with fine metal mesh.

The idea of giving the reader tips on how to grow stinging nettle will bring a smile, or more probably a grimace, to the face of most gardeners. However, it is an important foodplant and you will not find any cultural instructions in a gardening book! It is best grown from rootstocks rather than from seed. In February you can find young shoots just showing above ground in sheltered places. Dig out some roots about 4 or 5 inches long bearing the young shoots, and bury a handful in each flowerpot. Keep pruning the shoots so that they are never more than 3 inches high and by the end of March you will have strong roots with many green shoots that can be allowed to grow on. These will provide plenty of suitable young green leaves for your nymphalids – a small tortoiseshell, for example, will not lay on hoary old leaves. After the nettles have nourished the spring brood of caterpillars, cut them back in readiness for the later broods.

Although I began with the male and female in the breeding flowerpot, you may prefer to purchase chrysalids. These can be hatched out in emerging cages similar to those described in 'A Tropical Life Cycle'. In inclement weather the gap between the hatching of males and females may be longer than usual and it is therefore best to acquire at least ten pupae to increase the chances of having males and fresh females at the same time.

Pests and other Problems

You will have realized by now how vitally dependent your butterflies are on their nectar and foodplants. Unfortunately, the plants are host to many pests which affect their health and at worst may destroy them. Many of the generally used insecticides cannot be employed because of the risk of harming your butterflies. In my experience, the most dangerous pests that occur in the rather special conditions you have created are mealy bugs, scale insect, whitefly, red spider mite, aphids and sciarid flies. Except for the latter all are sap-suckers.

Mealy bugs, if unchecked, produce large colonies, which look like white powder, under leaves and around stems. Among their favourite host plants are banana, avocado, passion flower and oleander, but if present in epidemic proportions they are not at all fussy.

Scale insects, which look like tiny transparent military tanks, less than half the size of a ladybird, hook their feet and jaws into leaves and stems. They are particularly fond of *Citrus*, Mexican orange, *Hoya*, *Stephanotis* and oleander.

In very small numbers and provided all the affected plants are easily accessible, both these pests can be destroyed by wiping the plants' leaves and stems with cotton wool dipped in paraffin or methylated spirits – preferably outside the greenhouse. The plants should then be thoroughly sprayed with water to wash away the dead pests and the residue of your treatment.

If there is an epidemic, or if you have neither the time nor inclination to treat all your plants, there is a very effective method of biological control. This involves using as an ally a species of Australian ladybird *Cryptolaemus montrolizieri*, which is dark muddy red and black in colour. Its larvae, although larger, mimic those of mealy bugs, so it is important not to kill them in error. Ideally, the affected plants should be touching one another so that both adults and larvae can move from plant to plant in search of their prey.

Cryptolaemus (both adults and larvae) prefers mealy bugs but also attacks scale insects, particularly after the former have been wiped out. All stages of the butterflies are left strictly alone. This kind of control does take time but it is safe and effective. For a minor infestation, which is better treated by hand, it is an expensive remedy.

Whitefly, small moth-like insects, are resistant to most sprays and can survive a considerable range of temperature and humidity. They excrete a sugary substance, derived from the plant's sap, which coats the foliage and promotes the growth of a sooty mould. It is unsightly and prevents leaves from functioning properly. A well-known pest to all greenhouse gardeners, it occurs outside in sheltered spots, and has devastating results unless quickly controlled. It attacks *Lantana*, heliotrope, honeysuckle, *Buddleia*, milkweed, and *Verbena*; in large numbers its choice of plant is more cosmopolitan. It can be controlled by the minute parasitic chalcid wasp *Encarsia formosa*, which is more effective against low numbers of whitefly, thereby preventing a build-up of the pest, than against a large population. The wasp lays its eggs inside the developing whitefly larvae, the parasite instead of the whitefly emerges from the pupae.

The fungus *Verticillium lecanii* sometimes attacks whitefly and can be used as an alternative form of control. It would, however, be an expensive method for amateurs because it is only supplied in commercial quantities.

Red spider mite is another well-known pest in the greenhouse and, in a warm summer, can cause havoc in the garden. Its population can build up to such an extent that plants may be festooned with their webs which, under a magnifying glass, are seen to be a mass of minute greenish-red spiders and white eggs. Eventually, the leaves turn yellow and fall off. Soon after the London Butterfly House opened we had a severe infestation which started on the passion-flower vine and rapidly spread to other plants. It was controlled by the introduction of a minute predatory mite, *Phytoseiulus persimilis*. With the temperature not less than 60°F, new generations of this predator appeared at 10-day intervals and the red spider mite soon succumbed to its attacks. It is worth noting that the red spider mite dislikes high humidity, so if this condition can be maintained this pest will not be a problem.

All the biological controls mentioned have proved highly effective in the Butterfly House, which has apparently been free of the pests they control. I say 'apparently' because the pests must be present at least in very small numbers, otherwise their predators would die, allowing the pests once again to get out of hand. Several firms specialize in these biological controls, at least one of which (listed in an Appendix) supplies amateur packs of the insects required for controlling the above-mentioned pests.

Despite the fact that aphids do not thrive at high temperatures, they can be a problem in the greenhouse. Control can be achieved by spraying affected plants with a systemic chemical specific to aphids, and one such is Rapid (also sold under the brand names Pirimor or Pirimicarb). Experimental feeding of small tortoiseshell caterpillars on nettles treated with it produced no ill effects. However, it should be used very sparingly and with great care because, recently, it may have adversely affected a colony of heliconiids.

The same fungus that attacks whitefly also kills aphids, and luckily it is present in the London Butterfly House. The small papery tent-like structures that we see on some of the foliage are the remains of the fungus-infected aphids.

Sciarid fly larvae are another potentially dangerous pest. These small white maggots feed on the roots of a wide range of plants, especially those grown in pots. They are quite capable of killing seedlings and even mature plants. The adult flies resemble miniature houseflies with extra-long legs. This pest may be controlled by carefully watering the plants' growing medium with Sybol 2, Keristray or Picket. To be effective these products have to be ingested by the larvae within the soil, and so are harmless to the butterflies.

Thrips and leaf hoppers certainly damage some plants but they have not been serious pests in the Butterfly House. A predatory mite, not yet available to the amateur, has been used as a biological control for thrips, and the Glasshouse Crops Research Institute is doing valuable work on other forms of biological control for this and the leaf hopper. Among them are different kinds of fungi which specifically attack these two pests and thus are not harmful to other insects. No doubt they will eventually reach the marketplace.

If you cannot afford natural pest controls there is another comparatively satisfactory, and certainly economical method of controlling most soft-bodied plant pests in small flight areas. All you require is time, care, and ordinary washing-up liquid. Take all the potted plants from the flight cage on a warm day and, using a hand spray, soak the infected plants with a 1 per cent solution of the liquid. If possible, keep the plants separate from the butterflies for a couple of days and then thoroughly spray them with water to ensure that there is no residual deposit to kill the butterflies or caterpillars. If the plants in the greenhouse borders are infected, carefully spray a few plants at a time with the solution and then immediately tie polythene bags over them to prevent butterflies from coming into contact with them. After two days, remove the bags and thoroughly wash the plants with water.

In addition to the more serious insect pests dealt with above, there are a few others that deserve mention. Among these are ants, which are not too serious unless they have made a regular highway onto your hanging baskets, or if the caterpillar foodplants are unsleeved. They do, however, sometimes attack roosting or weak butterflies and carry off eggs and tiny caterpillars which, perhaps, you have not collected. Control them by putting Nippon on the ant runs, under a flowerpot so that the butterflies cannot get at it. The ants carry this substance back to the nest where it kills their queen, eventually causing the whole colony to perish. Some ant baits also kill earwigs, which can be persistent enemies, devouring eggs and small caterpillars. They are seldom seen since they hide in crevices and are only active at night.

Parasitic wasps and flies in the wild are particularly devastating. In the tropics there are numerous groups, including ichneumonids, chalcids, braconids and tachinids, all of which lay their eggs on, in, or near butterfly eggs, caterpillars or chrysalids, their larvae devouring the contents. You must catch and kill them whenever they appear in your greenhouse. Our native parasitic species are just as troublesome. Most insidious are the miniscule chalcid flies, partly because they are able to find their way through all but the finest netting. Their eggs are injected into butterfly eggs, the larvae devour the contents and eventually the adult parasites hatch and break out of the butterfly eggs to continue the cycle. If some of your larvae develop black patches under their skins, the chances are they have been attacked by an ichneumon. Later the fly larvae will find their way through the skin to form a cluster of silk cocoons on its outside. These too must be destroyed before they have had a chance to hatch and breed to continue their activities. Other native parasitic species lay their eggs inside the soft body of a newly formed chrysalis. I have seen individual *Pteromalus* parasites actually clinging to a fully grown swallowtail caterpillar waiting for pupation to take place so that they can lay their eggs.

All these parasites are relatively easily controlled by sleeving your caterpillars with very fine netting, and since you will usually have plenty of eggs, sufficient should escape the parasites' attention to ensure survival of your stock. Many tropical species do not seem to be troubled by our native parasites, possibly because they are specific to certain butterflies. However if you are breeding native butterflies you will have to be careful.

Spiders are very troublesome predators of both butterflies and caterpillars. The smallest can kill a caterpillar ten times its own size. If unsleeved, your caterpillars may be wiped out by a large spider population. Those that make webs are relatively easy to detect and kill but those that roam far and wide, like the hunting spider, are almost impossible to catch and kill by hand. In the London Butterfly House I have a pair of Chinese quails, which eat spiders as well as small insects like ants but seldom take caterpillars or peck at butterflies that have fallen to the ground or are roosting there. The quails rarely fly unless alarmed and so stay at ground level. In the absence of quails, which are only suitable for the larger greenhouse, your only solution is to scrutinize your foliage and all parts of the greenhouse regularly, and destroy the spiders and their nests by hand.

Slugs and snails revel in damp conditions and will do much damage to your plants if allowed to thrive. Some slugs are carnivorous and feed on eggs, caterpillars and even butterflies while they are resting at night. These creatures should be controlled by 'safe' pellets – that is, the type that dries up the slime on which slugs and snails rely for locomotion. The powder, Fertosan, works on the same principle and the makers say is harmless to other animals. 'Slug pubs' are effective traps; half fill jars with stale beer and sink to ground level in the border. Attracted by the beer, the slugs will drown.

If, one morning, you find some of your autumn collection of chrysalids missing from their emerging cage and a neat round hole in the netting, or some butterfly wings strewn about the ground, the culprit is a mouse. In a town it is likely to be a house mouse and elsewhere the long-tailed field mouse. Although your tropical butterflies may very well be the kinds that contain cyanide and mustard-oil poisons, the amount is inadequate to deter mice. Live traps are the best kind to use but if unobtainable you will have to use the spring sort or, taking suitable precautions, poison.

Leaving the world of animal pests we come to the most unpleasant enemies of all: the bacteria, viruses and fungi. Sooner or later these

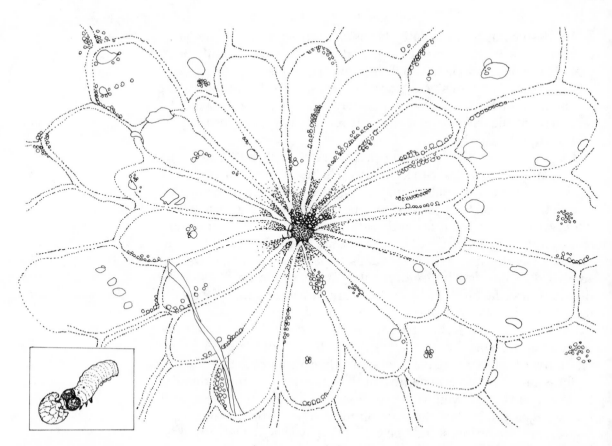

A drawing, based on an electron micrograph, of a small part of a pine-beauty moth eggshell covered with debris. The largest particles are fungal spores; the smaller, regular ones in the ribbing are viruses. These are protected by a crystalline coat that enables them to survive for long periods outside living tissue. As a guide to the scale of the drawing, the inset shows a pine-beauty caterpillar about 6 to 7 times life size eating its eggshell

unseen enemies may wipe out most of your butterflies. These pathogens are present in varying concentrations in the intestines of caterpillars, chrysalids and adult butterflies, on eggshells, the leaves of the foodplant, the caterpillar skin or chrysalis case, and amongst the scales on the butterflies' wings and in their droppings. They are such small organisms that they float around everywhere in the atmosphere and can only be avoided in sterile laboratory conditions.

Because they are unseen they tend to be ignored by amateur entomologists until the symptoms appear, when it is often too late. Baby caterpillars shrivel and die; large caterpillars suddenly go limp and hang by their prolegs, oozing a foul black liquid; others 'freeze' to twigs while white moulds spread along their flanks; a chrysalis turns black and slowly dissolves in an evil smelling soup. Whatever the symptom, you must destroy all caterpillars that have been in close contact with the victim. Do not become too discouraged by these difficulties, for these pathogens will usually only multiply to a level where they are capable of killing caterpillars, in conditions that are overcrowded and unfavourable or unhygenic. Healthy caterpillars are capable of withstanding the attacks of many of the less virulent organisms, whereas weak caterpillars, perhaps from stocks debilitated by attacks on previous generations, will succumb. Caterpillars kept at below optimum temperatures are very often lost because the bacteria or virus develops more quickly than they do.

Many entomologists wrongly blame 'in-breeding', thinking that this weakens the strain and promotes such infections. This was a view I held for many years, because wild-collected chrysalids or silk moth cocoons always seemed so much more vigorous, fatter and healthier than my second or third generation home-bred stocks, and they lived far longer.

The real reason was explained to me by a professional entomologist, Claude Rivers. Most of the bought chrysalids are bred outside, in their country of origin. In the wild an infected caterpillar is usually isolated – the female butterflies having hundreds of acres in which to lay their eggs. Furthermore, the microscopic organisms are washed into the soil by successive rainstorms and blown away by gales. The majority of chrysalids are therefore disease free, and there is no doubt that in the wild pathogenetic infections are relatively rare.

In the comparatively crowded conditions of captivity there is the danger of a built-up of pathogens. New stocks of healthy butterflies will live their allotted span but successive generations will tend to succumb in increasing numbers.

What can the amateur do to prevent or cure such pestilence? Here, a small greenhouse or conservatory can be an advantage. A thorough dousing of the staging, the glass, the capillary matting, all the breeding cages, in fact the whole of the inside of the greenhouse and its equipment, with a weak solution of Jeyes, Milton, or similar disinfectant fluid will destroy nearly all the offending organisms – cutting them down to levels which can be withstood by healthy caterpillars. The greenhouse should be so treated at least twice a year, and breeding cages, sleeves and ancillary equipment each time they are used. If you close the flight area for the winter you can do the job thoroughly at least once a year. In all cases, the livestock should be removed first and only replaced once the disinfectant has been washed away with clean water. Another safety measure is to store foodplants away from the flight area so that they are not infected by the residents. The caterpillars will then start life on uninfected foliage.

Since these infections are contracted at egg hatching time, if you continue to be troubled, the butterfly eggs themselves may be surface sterilized (see Appendix for details).

As soon as a caterpillar hatches it eats its eggshell, thereby ingesting most of the material adhering to it including quantities of injurious pathogens which then develop in the tissues of the growing caterpillar. If its foodplant is similarly covered the level of infection may become too great – the caterpillar then dies. Pathogens disrupt and burst the cells, and in some diseases the larva liquefies thereby dispersing millions of particles, spreading the disease even further. Susceptibility to infection decreases with the age of the larva. If you start with clean, uninfected eggs, the caterpillars start life healthy and are much more likely to survive contact with the viruses and bacteria which they inevitably ingest via their foodplant.

With all these agents around, I was, therefore, puzzled to find that my postmen and common mormons seemed to continue breeding while other species died out. I found the answer when I visited Brian Gardiner, a professional entomologist. He has bred large white butterflies in his garden shed for over 20 years, supplying stock to schools and laboratories. I was expecting to find immaculately clean cages, scrubbed and sterilized work surfaces and hardly a speck of dust. Not a bit of it. Brian Gardiner makes a virtue of rearing at high densities from egg to chrysalis without cleaning out his cages. From time to time, as epidemics have struck, he has lost up to 98% of his entire stock, but there were always survivors. He bred from these and over the years has produced a strain resistant to almost every known disease. Large whites, of course, are very common, as is their foodplant, so he can afford to be ruthless in the creation of a resistant strain. These methods are not really appropriate for tropical butterflies but by accident I, too, had bred resistant strains of postmen and common mormons – and so might you.

Another problem you may have to face is a cut in the supply of electricity. You may find, for example, several postman butterflies are on the floor, weak from lack of food, perhaps being carried off by a gang of ants, or a lime butterfly on the staging caught by a hunting spider. Eventually, the power is restored and you should reset the time clock to compensate. Raising the temperature will get things going again. Soon, most of the butterflies will be flying and feeding quite normally but perhaps two of the postmen and one lime but-

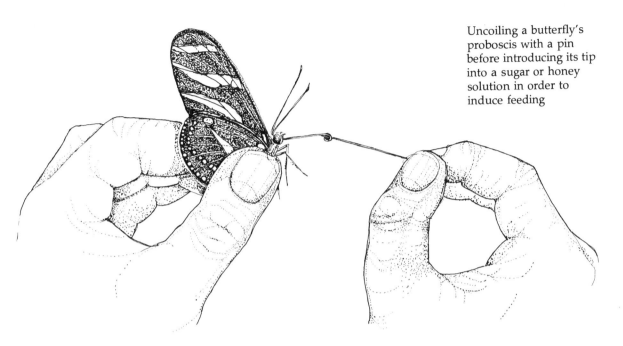

Uncoiling a butterfly's
proboscis with a pin
before introducing its tip
into a sugar or honey
solution in order to
induce feeding

terfly might be fluttering feebly and unable to take off. With a feather
touch you should take them by the wings and put them on the
flowers, when it is likely that at least some will start feeding and
become airborne in about half an hour.

It sometimes happens that when a butterfly gets caught for a long
period in a cold spot by the door, it gets so weak from hunger that it is
unable to fly and feed. In this case they can be hand fed. Place the feet
so that they are in contact with the honey- or sugar-water solution in
one of the tubes on the feeding table. Push the blunt end of a pin
away from the head to uncoil the proboscis, placing its tip into the
solution. Invariably the butterfly will start feeding and often will gain
enough strength to survive. If, during the winter, you are short of
nectar and your charges will not use the butterfly table, you can keep
them going, sometimes for weeks, by this means.

Many of you will be unable to afford the heating bills for maintain-
ing the correct temperatures during the winter months, and low light
levels and lack of nectar flowers may also worry you. At the end of
October you may have tropical species still on the go when you wish
to close down. It is best to destroy the eggs and any immature
caterpillars of those species that cannot overwinter (most caterpillars,
unless kept warm, will die anyway). If you have a number of nearly

full grown ones or you cannot bring yourself to destroy them you can always rear them to the chrysalis stage in a heated room in your house. But remember that the conditions will be dry compared with the greenhouse and you will need to spray them frequently or place a tray of water or wet gravel next to the cage. As for the remaining live butterflies and the chrysalids you are not keeping, I suggest you advertise in the bulletins of one of the entomological clubs and give them to a member who is keeping his greenhouse on the go during the winter. In return he may well agree to give you some interesting eggs or chrysalids the next spring. If you have a healthy colony of one of the long-lived heliconiid species, a college or laboratory may well take them on the same understanding. Some of the butterfly houses may be grateful for them, for even those which close for the winter always maintain small heated enclosures to keep a breeding nucleus.

If you cannot bear to lose your butterflies, I have found that some species can survive our winter. Although truly tropical butterflies breed continuously, some behave like temperate species, and go through a 'resting' period either as eggs, caterpillars, most usually as chrysalids, or as adult butterflies. Others may be induced to go through such a period, or to extend their normal resting period, by putting them in cool conditions. Care is required, however, as prolonged periods will cause the death of some semi-tropical chrysalids; others are 'programmed' by the conditions they experience as caterpillars to hatch after a certain interval whatever the temperatures they subsequently experience as chrysalids. In the London Butterfly House the Paris peacock (*Papilio paris*), reckoned to be a tropical species at least in part of its range, has overwintered as a chrysalis. So have the common mormon (*P. polytes*), the dark mormon (*P. protenor*) and the common bluebottle (*Graphium sarpedon*). All these were warmed up in early March and hatched by the end of that month.

The Palearctic and Nearctic species listed in the chart tend to have, in all or part of their range, a winter resting period or hibernation. Also, some species from warm regions with distinct wet and dry seasons tend to undergo a dry season resting period or aestivation until the onset of the next rains.

Winter is a time for cleaning and sterilizing the greenhouse and its contents, mending broken equipment, cleaning plant pots, cages and sleeves, taking cuttings and sowing seeds of various plants you will need, including any new varieties. It is also a convenient time to place your order for livestock.

Appendix 1: Native Butterflies (partly after P. Whalley)
The species that are most likely to be attracted to your garden

On the wing (months)

Names (after Carter 1982)	Range in UK	Principal caterpillar foodplants	Nectar plants	1	2	3	4	5	6	7	8	9	10	11	12	Over-winters as	Broods
brimstone (*Gonepteryx rhamni*)	C & S Eng, Wa, (Sc), rare N	buckthorn, alder buckthorn	thistles, knapweeds, *Aubrieta*, valerian	*	*	*	*	*			*	*	*	*	*	adult	1
small white (*Pieris rapae*)	UK	cabbage, cauliflower, broccoli, rape, garlic mustard, winter-cress, cleome, nasturtium (*Tropaeolum*) mignonette	*Arabis, Aubrieta*				*	*	*	*	*	*	*			chrysalis	2/3 may overlap
large white (*Pieris brassicae*)	UK		*Arabis, Aubrieta*				*	*	*	*	*	*	*			chrysalis	2/3
green-veined white (*Pieris napi*)	most UK, less com. far N	garlic mustard, winter-cress, horse-raddish	Cruciferae				*	*	*	*	*					chrysalis	1/2
orange tip (*Anthocharis cardamines*)	most UK, less com. in N	garlic mustard, dames-violet lady's-smock	Cruciferae				*	*	*							chrysalis	1
wall (*Lasiommata megera*)	C & S Eng, Wa, N Eng to S Sc	grasses	bramble, valerian					*	*	*	*	*				caterpillar	2/3
meadow brown (*Maniola jurtina*)	UK	grasses, esp. *Poa*	hayfield flora, *Buddleia*, thistles Umbelliferae						*	*	*	*				caterpillar	1
gatekeeper (*Pyronia tithonus*)	Eng & Wa, less com. N Eng, (?Sc)	grasses, e.g. *Poa; Milium effusum*	Hayfield flora, *Buddleia*							*	*					caterpillar	1
small heath (*Coenonympha pamphilus*)	Eng, Wa, Sc	grasses, e.g. *Poa; Nardus stricta*	hayfield flora, valerian					*	*	*	*	*				caterpillar	1/2
ringlet (*Aphantopus hyperantus*)	most Eng & Wa, less N Eng & Sc	grasses, e.g. *Poa; Milium effusum*; sometimes sedges (*Carex*)	hayfield flora							*	*					caterpillar	1
speckled wood (*Pararge aegeria*)	UK (N, Sc)	grasses, esp. couches (*Elymus*)	various, inc. bramble; honeydew from leaves				*	*	*		*	*				caterpillar and/or chrysalis	
small skipper (*Thymelicus sylvestris*)	most Eng & Wa (far N Eng, Sc)	grasses, e.g. *Deschampsia, Holcus*	hayfield flora							*	*	*				caterpillar	1
dingy skipper (*Erynnis tages*)	Eng, Wa, local Sc & Ire	bird's-foot trefoil	knapweeds & other Compositae					*	*	*	*	*	*			caterpillar	1/2 2 in S
large skipper (*Ochlodes venata*)	most UK; commonest S & C Eng; found S Sc	grasses, e.g. *Festuca, Poa*; rushes (*Juncus*)	hayfield flora						*	*	*					caterpillar	1/2
common blue (*Polyommatus icarus*)	UK	small Leguminosae, esp. *Lotus, Trifolium, Vicia*	hayfield flora						*	*	*	*	*			caterpillar	1 gen. N, 2–3 S
small copper (*Lycaena phlaeas*)	UK	docks and common sorrel	hayfield flora, Compositae						*	*	*	*	*			caterpillar	3, 4 gen. S
holly blue (*Celastrina argiolus*)	C & S Eng, Wa, less com. further N; rec. Sc	holly, ivy	*Cotoneaster*, ivy, holly				*	*	*	*	*	*				chrysalis	2–3
small tortoiseshell (*Aglais urticae*)	UK	stinging nettles	Michaelmas daisy, *Sedum spectabile, Buddleia*	*	*	*	*	*			*	*	*	*	*	adult	2
peacock (*Inachis io*)	UK, less com. Sc	stinging nettles	as above	*	*	*	*	*			*	*	*	*	*	adult	1
red admiral (*Vanessa atalanta*)	UK	stinging nettles	as above and fallen fruit	(•)	(•)	(•)	*	*			*	*	(•)	(•)	(•)	migrant and adult	1
painted lady (*Cynthia cardui*)	UK, but more com. in S & C Eng, Wa	creeping thistle, burdocks, globe artichoke, occ. stinging nettles	thistles, valerian						*	*	*	*	*			occ. as adult	1
comma (*Polygonia c-album*)	S & C Eng, Wa; less com. N	hop, occ. stinging nettles	as small tortoise-shell	*	*	*	*	*			*	*	*	*		adult	2

C	Central	S	South	Wa	Wales	inc.	including
E	East	Sc	Scotland	com.	common	occ.	occasionally
Eng	England	(Sc)	not Scotland	esp.	especially	rec.	recorded
N	North	W	West	gen.	generally		

(*) rarely seen but recorded
Butterflies are on the wing earlier in the South and Midlands, and have more broods in good years than in N England & Scotland

1/2 one or two broods per year – one in the north, two in the south (depending on the weather)

Appendix 2: Tropical Butterflies
A selection of relatively easy-to-breed species

Family, scientific & vernacular names/regions	Caterpillar foodplants	Notes
PAPILIONIDE		
Battus philenor pipevine swallowtail Nearctic	*Aristolochia* spp., inc. Dutchman's pipe & birthwort; *Polygonum* spp., wild ginger (*Asarum*)	ow. in part of range; mimicked by *P. troilus*
Pachiliopta aristolochiae common rose Oriental	*Aristolochia* spp., inc. Dutchman's pipe, birthwort & *A. tagala*	cb., in wild, fond of *Lantana* blossom; mimicked by a fem. form of *P. polytes*
Papilio polytes common mormon Oriental, Palearctic	*Citrus, Choisya ternata, Skimmia japonica* & other Rutaceae	lll.; cb. in warm conditions; can be induced to ow. as chrs., if kept cool
P. protenor (demetrius) darm mormon Oriental, Palearctic	ditto, also African marigold foliage	as *P. polytes*
P. xuthus swallowtail Oriental, Palearctic	*Citrus, Choisya ternata, Skimmia japonica, Poncirus trifoliata* & Amur cork tree & other Rutaceae	will ow. as chrys.; similar markings to our native swallowtail
P. demoleus lime butterfly Oriental, Australasian	as *P. xuthus*; also African marigold & cosmos foliage	see pp. 83–85, 90–93
P. memnon great mormon Oriental, Palearctic	as *P. xuthus*	several fem. forms; chrys. will ow. if kept cool
P. paris Paris peacock Oriental	as *P. xuthus*; also willow & sallow	normally cb.; chrys. will ow. at least for a few months if kept cool
P. polymnestor Oriental	*Citrus* & other Rutaceae	Sri Lanka & S. India only; cb.
P. glaucus tiger swallowtail Nearctic	tulip tree, wild cherry, willow, ash, birch & hop tree	2–3 broods per year; will ow. as chrys.
P. polyxenes palamedes swallowtail Nearctic	red bay, sassafras, sweet bay, occasionally accepts avocado	will ow. as chrys. emerging late Feb. onwards if introduced to warm conditions
P. troilus spice bush swallowtail Nearctic	as for *P. polyxenes*; also prickly ash (*Zanthoxylum americanum*), try other Rutaceae	as for *P. polyxenes*
P. thoas thoas swallowtail Neotropical	*Citrus*, also some Lauraceae	usually cb.
P. helenus red Helen Oriental, Palearctic	as *P. xuthus*	normally cb.; lll.
P. bianor Chinese peacock Oriental, Palearctic	as *P. xuthus*	stock from cooler parts of range, e.g. Japan, will ow. as chrys.
P. aegeus orchard swallowtail Australasian	*Citrus, Choisya ternata* & other Rutaceae	normally cb.
P. demodocus Christmas butterfly Ethiopian	*Citrus, Choisya ternata*; also African marigold & cosmos foliage	similar but larger than *P. demoleus*
Graphium agamemnon tailed jay Palearctic	*Annona* spp. inc. cultivated custard apple (*A. squamosa*)	will ow. in cool conditions; a. fond of mud puddles & dung as well as nectar; custard apple easily grown from stones taken from its fruit
SATYRIDAE		
Caligo memnon giant owl butterfly Neotropical	banana, *Strelitzia*, lilies & other monocotyledons	most active dawn & dusk; a. feeds on rotting fruit, rather than flowers; lives 3 months or more; likes bananas, grapes, pineapple; cater. feed up slowly, perhaps over a period of months during cool spells
DANAIDAE		
Danaus plexippus monarch or milkweed Neotropical, Nearctic	most spp. of milkweed, *Calotropis gigantea, Aranjia hortorum*	a. will mate readily after a few days, even in smallish flight area; cater. eat large amounts of foliage; autumn generation hibernates when atmosphere humid, just...

Species	Food plant	Notes
D. chrisippus plain tiger Oriental, Ethiopian, Australasian	most spp. of milkweed, *Calotropis gigantea, C. procera*	cb.; easily mated; cater. similar but smaller than monarch
Euploea core common crow Oriental, Ethiopian, Australasian	*Nerium oleander, Ficus* spp. inc. *F. benjamina*; milkweeds	cater. tend to be canabalistic – keep well spaced; cb.
E. mulciber striped blue crow Oriental	*Nerium oleander*, milkweeds	notes as for common crow
Idea leuconoe greater tree nymph Oriental	*Tylophora ovata*; try other spp. of Asclepiadaceae, also Apocynaceae	a. very long lived; lll; also seek alkaloids; will occasionally feed on dung as well as flowers

NYMPHALDAE

Species	Food plant	Notes
Heliconis melpomene postman Neotropical	*Passiflora caerulea*; try other smooth-leaved *Passiflora*	a. exceptionally, live to 8 mths; need pollen as well as nectar; lll.; cb.; mated fem. smells diff. from unmated one; young cater. prefer tendril tips & young tender leaves
H. charitonius zebra Neotropical	as for *H. melpomene*	as for *H. melpomene*, but tolerates cooler conditions
Agraulis vanillae Gulf fritillary Neotropical	ditto	easy sp.; can be so successful it will eat all your *Passiflora* & so likely to destroy other *Heliconius* spp.; tolerates cooler conditions than postman
Hypolimnas bolina common eggfly Oriental, Ethiopian, Australasian	many spp. of Amaranthaceae, Acanthaceae, Portulacaceae; reared on sweet potato foliage & stinging nettle in captivity	long lived; in captivity in cool conditions it goes into a sort of semi-hibernation, waking on warm days to feed on fermenting fruit
H. misippus diadem butterfly Most warmer parts of world	Acanthaceae & Portulacaceae; reared on bear's-breech (*Acanthus mollis*) & stinging nettle in captivity	enjoys rotting fruit; behaves similarly to *H. bolina*; colour of sexes is different – fem. mimics plain tiger, male has black wings with white blotches
Kaniska canace Oriental	Smilacaceae inc. *Smilax china*	montane sp.; tolerates cooler temp.; does not like lll.; cb.
Phalanta phalantha small leopard Oriental, Australasian	weeping willow (*Salix babylonica*), *Flacourtia indica*	larvae develop very quickly – c. 1 week from hatching to chrys. if kept warm enough; cb.
Precis orithya blue pansy Oriental, Australasian	snapdragon, black-eyed Susan (*Thunbergia alata*) & other Acanthaceae	cb., but larvae grow very slowly in cool conditions
Acraea nocoda Ethiopian	stinging nettles, thistles	eggs laid in batches; cater. feed gregariously; a. weak fliers; tolerate small flight area; cb.

LYCAENIDAE

Species	Food plant	Notes
Lampides boeticus pea blue or long-tailed blue Oriental, Palearctic, Australasian	many Leguminosae; takes lupins, garden & sweet peas in captivity	eggs laid on flowers in which young larvae tunnel, later to feed on developing pods & seeds; pupate on or under ground; has reached Eng. as a rare migrant

PIERIDAE

Species	Food plant	Notes
Catopsilia florella African migrant Ethiopian, Oriental, Palearctic	*Cassia* spp., *Acacia* spp., buckthorn; try false acacia	also in Canary Is.; most *Cassia* spp. easily grown from seed; cb.
Eurema hecabe common grass yellow Oriental, Australasian	spp. of *Cassia, Caesalpinia, Cratoxylon, Albizzia* & others	very common throughout its range; fond of mud puddles as well as flowers
Hebomia glaucippe great orange tip Oriental, Palearctic	*Cleome spinosa* & other Capparidaceae; cabbage, rape & other Cruciferae	ow. in part of range; visits mud puddles as well as flowers; fem. has rows of black spots on upper wing edges; *C. spinosa* easily grown from seed

Australasian region: Australia, New Zealand, New Guinea & adjacent islands
Ethiopian region: Africa south of the Sahara
Nearctic region: N. America north of tropical Mexico
Neotropical region: tropical Mexico south to Cape Horn
Oriental region: India, Sri Lanka, Pakistan, S. China, S.E. Asia & Sulawesi
Palearctic region: Europe & Asia N. of Himalayas, & N. of Sahara

a.	adult(s)	fem.	female
cater.	caterpillar(s)	lll.	tolerate(s) low light levels
cb.	continuously brooded	lvs.	leaves
chrys.	chrysalis	ow.	overwinters

Appendix 3: The Cultivation of Butterfly Flowers

Wild Flowers and Grass Mixtures

The Nature Conservancy have produced a list of standard mixtures of grasses and native wild flowers suitable for growing in gardens, fields, road verges and parks. These are now on the market and can be obtained from the seedsmen given in Appendix 6.

If you are going to seed down a piece of bare ground you will need to buy approximately 15 kg for one acre, costing about £44 per kg (John Chambers' 1982 price list). If, on the other hand, you plan to harrow seed directly into existing sward, you can dispense with the grass and employ only a mixture of wild flower seed. In this case you can use 5 kg to the acre, costing approximately the same amount per kg. You can, of course, ask the seedsman to prepare a mixture of your own choice. Or, for example, if you wish to increase the proportion of oxeye daisies in your mixture you can say so, and ask him to include ragged-robin or kidney vetch or whatever else you fancy listed in his catalogue.

The Management of Wild Flowers and Grass

Sowing Seed mixtures of grass and wild flowers should be sown about the end of October. They can also be sown successfully in the spring, but are less likely to flower the same summer.

Prepare a seed bed as described on p. 46. If you wish to sow a flowering grass patch on a bare corner of the garden, or between fruit trees, or instal a small field, mix the flower seed and grass together and broadcast by hand. Or sow the grass first and then sow the flower seed mixed well with damp sand.

If sowing direct into existing sward (whether a field, lawn or bank), rake first with a wire rake, then broadcast the seed, rake in the opposite direction and walk lightly over the area (see also p. 41). If sown indoors, in pans, special treatments to remove germination inhibitors are necessary (see p. 41). Instructions on the packet will advise you what to do.

Storage If you have to store seed before sowing (for a short period – the germination rate drops off after 8 to 10 months) keep it in a cool, dry place, preferably in a flat, covered tray with a ball of napthalene in the corner. Protect the storage area from mice and ants!

Fertilizer Never use fertilizer for growing wild flowers. Fertilizers will ensure that the vigorous grasses in mixtures swamp the flowering 'weeds'. Wild flowers prefer poor soil. In the kitchen garden they grow too much foliage if the soil is rich. If you think your soil is too fertile you can remove the top layer and use it for your vegetables.

Cutting and Mowing The Nature Conservancy advise cutting with an Allen autoscythe at a height of 8 – 10 cm eight weeks after sowing on bare soil, and for the first year, cut every two months thereafter to give the wild flowers a chance against weeds and tough grass. But this is a regime for road verges

and parks or fields. In a garden, where the sown area is relatively tiny, hand weeding of the larger weeds (dock, thistle, fat-hen, etc.) is best and no cutting before the autumn. Cut during September, and if the growth is strong, mow again in early November. Add seedlings, and rake or harrow in additional seed after the first cut. When sowing directly into sward no weeding is necessary. You may find that many wild flowers fail to bloom the first season, but do not be discouraged. They will probably flower the next year.

Seedlings Sow and grow cowslips, primroses, violets, harebells, buttercups, oxeye daisies and poppies in rows in your kitchen garden as if they were lettuces (see p. 41). Weed assiduously round them; transplant healthy seedlings, nine months old, into existing sward in Sep. or Oct. They can also be transplanted in the early spring (at 14 months) during a mild spell. Plant the poppies in bare patches only (there always are some!). You can add to the number of species grown in the kitchen garden if time and space permit. Do not forget that hand weeding is necessary and time consuming. These wild flowers cannot compete with arable weeds.

Seed gathering from plants grown in the kitchen garden Wild flower seed ripens very late; most collecting is done in late August and September. We have found the most satisfactory and quickest method is to cut the plants a few inches above ground and spread the stems on polythene sheets to dry in the greenhouse or on the kitchen floor. When dry, the seeds must be separated from the dried-up remains. If you were going to sell the seed it would have to be cleaned by passing it through a series of finer and finer sieves. But for your own use it need not be prepared so carefully – you do not require an exact weight of the sample and a bit of chaff or trash will do no harm. If you are gathering seed from road verges or a derelict airfield, a plastic bag can be held beneath the dried head of the plant (only collect from very common species) which is nipped off with a pair of scissors. This is less wasteful than pulling off seedheads by hand and also less time consuming. But do not keep the seed in the plastic bags for they become mildewed – dry them in a saucer or similar container.

Wild Flowers

Cardamine pratensis (lady's smock)
Perennial; common in moist meadows and along streams; white and pale mauve flowers. Although less than 1 ft high, growing in the wild the pod is more than 1 in long, but contains disappointingly few seeds. Multiplies vegetatively from buds on the leaves. A lawn can be mown continuously for 20 years or more, but if cutting ceases a sheet of flowers can appear in the area. Forms a bushy plant, free flowering at least the first year in the kitchen garden, but grows best in soggy soil. Pollinated by the orange tip butterfly: also larval food plant. Two distinct races in the U.K.

Chrysanthemum leucanthemum (oxeye daisy)
The flowers are borne on long stems rising from rosettes of leaves close to the ground. There are a number of genetically distinct strains, and also environmental variations. Seed not infrequently lie dormant for the winter and only germinate

the following spring. Barely cover with soil if sowing in the kitchen garden. An average yield for one plant is about 2700 fruits. Very easy to grow either from seed harrowed or raked into sward, or from transplanted seedlings, and extremely attractive either in early green hay or late brown grass. Butterflies visit them frequently, but they are not a first choice. The same applies to the corn marigold which was formerly a very common weed in cornfields – introduced with foreign wheat seed, especially from Russia. Modern methods of screening have reduced it almost to vanishing point, like the cornflower and corncockle.

Cirsium arvense (creeping thistle)
A root-stock perennial with annual stems 3–4 ft high. Very prickly. The small mauve flowers are deliciously scented and most attractive to butterflies. Can be grown all too easily from seed – usually unintentionally. (Note: this species is on the Ministry of Agriculture's proscribed list.) Flowers throughout the summer, including Sept. Keep under control! Found in waste places and cultivated grounds accompanying agriculture in all parts of the world.

Lonicera periclymenum (common honeysuckle)
All species of *Lonicera* like a good moist soil and flower best in full sunshine, but they grow attractively and freely in shady woodland. Easily propagated by seed or cuttings. *L periclymenum* flowers in summer and late summer, and by using different varieties and other species the flowering season can be from May to Sept.

Lotus corniculatus (bird's-foot trefoil)
A common sun-loving, perennial member of the pea family. Spreads vegetatively and withstands heavy grazing and trampling. Flowers and fruits in grazed turf. Pods about 1 in long. Grown easily from seed; rubbing seed between sandpaper improves germination. Nectar source and food plant of blue butterflies and burnet moths. Flowers all summer.

Prunella vulgaris (selfheal)
A perennial with branching prostrate stem from which arise leafy shoots bearing handsome purple flowers. On a lawn it flowers when only a few inches high, but in the kitchen garden is a stout plant with each flowering stem reaching 9 in. Blooms throughout the summer. Very easy to grow; it prefers damp calcareous soils. There are two types, a small female and a larger bisexual plant. The seeds, difficult to separate from their capsules, pass through the intestines of birds unharmed and germinate successfully. Sow in the kitchen garden, like carrot seed, and in pots; introduced very successfully as seed and seedlings into dense sward on steep banks. Sunny situations preferred. Pollinated by butterflies.

Silene pratensis & *S. dioica* (white & red campion)
Annual, biennial or short-lived perennials. The white campion opens in the evening, emitting a sweet scent, the red campion in the morning. They grow well on both alluvial and heavy clay or chalky soil in waste and arable places. The red campion prefers shady sites, including woodlands with an open canopy, while the white campion prefers a sunny situation. Separate male and female plants growing up to 2 ft; one female plant produces up to 15,000 seeds. Germination intermittent and can be initially low and delayed for one or two years after sowing. Sow Feb.–May and Aug.–Nov. Both pollinated by butterflies and moths.

Sonchus arvensis (perennial corn sow-thistle)
A common perennial (sometimes annual) wasteland weed, with handsome bright yellow fragment flowers arranged in loose panicles. Stems 2–3 ft tall. A useful nectar source in the autumn and very decorative if sown in the right place. Seeds with parachute-like silky white hairs, wind distributed, but can remain dormant for 10 years or more in the soil.

Taraxacum officinale (dandelion)
Dandelions need no description. Their flowers close completely at night, but open in response to light and warmth. Reproduction of viable fruits is without fertilization (apomictic), but distribution (by parachute) is like that of normally produced seeds. Flourishes in a diversity of soils, especially heavy clays with a chalky element. Extremely easy to grow from seed with an immediate 90% germination. Barely cover with soil. Sow at any time. Seedlings flower the following year. About 2000 seeds per plant. Also propagated from portions of the thick, bitter tasting tap root. Not only a source of nectar for butterflies but a food plant of the garden tiger and its relatives the ermine moths.

Trifolium & *Vicia spp* (clovers & vetches)
Annuals and perennials of meadows and waste ground with flowers of various colours. Clovers are fairly low growing and the vetches are scramblers. Most require open positions and reasonable soil. Can be grown from seed (but some vetches need scarification before sowing). Good nectar sources and some of the smaller species are the foodplant of the common blue caterpillar.

Garden Flowers
Aster spp. (Michaelmas daisies)
Common name strictly belongs to *A. novi-belgii* but used for many other species. All are hardy herbaceous perennials, easily cultivated in ordinary garden soils. Late summer to autumn flowering. Best divided in spring. Endless varieties are available, but the older, single kinds are more attractive to butterflies. *A. foliaceus* ssp. *cusickii* is a fine plant (from woodland places in the Rocky Mountains) for butterflies. Can be propagated from seed as well as division.

Aubrieta deltoidea
Evergreen perennial rock plants, with flowers ranging from deep purple to rose-lilac. Thrive in any deep rich loam in the sun and grow well in walls and dry banks. Can be grown easily from seed sown in Feb. or March. Old plants can be divided after flowering. The long, slender branches may be layered at any time after flowering and if covered with sandy leaf mould they root freely and can be separated and planted for spring flowering. Also, cutting can be taken in June – July. Attractive to over-wintered butterflies.

Buddleia davidii (butterfly bush)
Grows well in almost any soil, in cities and by the sea, and in all types of gardens, also against the wall of a house. Flourishes in full sun. Commonly lilac, but can be obtained in other colours, ranging from dark purple to white. Grown easily from seed, or cuttings in Oct. Prune hard in March.

Flowers in late July–Aug. Different varieties can extend the flowering season from early May to Sept. Side branches flower late in the season if the dead flowers are removed.
Callistephus sinensis (Chinese aster)
A large-flowered annual species about 1–1½ ft tall with showy blooms of many colours. Very easy to grow from seed in any ordinary garden soil. The mixed race best for attracting butterflies. Irresistible to the small tortoiseshell in late summer.
Centranthus ruber (red valerian; soldiers' pride)
Hardy perennial with blueish-green leaves and tiny pink flowers. Easily grown in all ordinary soils – in gravel, cracks in walls, flowerbeds, etc. June to late Aug. Readily increased by division and seed.
Chrysanthemum rubellum 'Clara Curtis'
Hardy perennial, 2½–3 ft tall. Framed with pink rays. Flowers in mid or late Oct. Grows easily in good garden soils, in open border; sow where it is to flower. Readily increased by division. Extremely attractive to small tortoiseshells.
Eupatorium spp (hemp-agrimony)
A large genus of many species. Mostly perennial. The nectar of their flowers is the source of sexual attractants for various butterflies. Our native *E. cannabinum* is easily grown in ordinary garden soil and in a wild garden. Increase by division.
Iberis spp (candytuft)
A genus of hardy and half-hardy annuals and sub-shrubs. White, purple and mauve. Grows in well-drained ordinary soil and magnificently along gravel paths, preferring the dry soil and lack of competition (well spread out). Autumn sowing of the annuals (*I. umbellata* being one of the best) produces spring flowers while March and April sowing give summer and autumn flowers. Perennial spp. raised from cuttings.
Lavandula spica (old English or common lavender)
Easily grown shrub in any reasonable friable soil – calcareous loam or sandy soil, well drained. Likes a sunny situation. Darker coloured forms are available. Propagation easy by means of cutting in late summer. Grows to a height of 3–4 ft.
Ligularia (=*Senecio*) *clivorum* (giant-leaved ragwort)
Herbaceous perennial. Grows well and aggressively in a free moist soil but a little peat dug in is a help. Propagate by division either in spring or summer (July–Aug.). Huge leaves 10–20 in wide, and grows 3–5 ft high. Makes good ground cover. Large yellow flowers.

Michaelmas daisies see *Aster* spp

Rubus fruticosus (blackberry; bramble) *R. idaeus* (raspberry)
Hardy deciduous shrubs. Growing freely in any good garden soil. Brambles are easily propagated by tip layers – seed takes longer. Some of the cultivated American blackberries are very attractive.
Sedum spectabile ('ice plant')
A sturdy, tough perennial that will thrive almost anywhere, but prefers a loamy soil. 10–18 in tall. Pink flowers. Sept. – Oct. Well adapted to pot culture; suitable for window sills. Easily propagated from seed, cutting or division of tufts in the spring. (Do not grow the darker red forms such as 'Autumn Joy', 'Brilliant' etc., which are not so attractive to butterflies.)

Verbena spp (vervain)
Annual and perennial. Most species suffer in hard winters. Require rich soil in full sun. Easily propagated, from seed sown in early spring. Various heights up to 5 ft Flowers generally in the scarlet to purple range. *V. bonariensis*, the tallest, most popular as butterfly nectar source. Propagate by root division, cuttings in spring or seed.

Appendix 4: Nectar Sources

Wild Flowers (Nomenclature: Keble Martin, 1972)

Vernacular name/Scientific name	Flowering period
alder buckthorn *Frangula alnus*	May – June
betony *Betonica officinalis*	June – Sept.
blackthorn *Prunus spinosa*	March – April
bladder campion *Silene vulgaris*	May – Aug.
bluebell *Endymion non-scriptus*	May
Bramble (blackberry) *Rubus* spp.	May – Sept.
bryony, white and black *Bryonia dioica;*	
Tamus communis	May – Aug.
bugle *Ajuga reptans*	May – July
buttercups *Ranunculus* spp.	April – Sept.
carline thistle *Carlina vulgaris*	July – Sept.
cat's-ears *Hypochoeris* spp.	May – Oct.
cinquefoils *Potentilla* spp.	April – Sept.
colt's-foot *Tusilago farfara*	March
comfreys *Symphytum* spp.	May – Aug.
common valerian *Valeriana officinalis*	June – Sept.
cornflower *Centaurea cyanus*	June – Aug.
cowslip *Primula veris*	April – May
creeping thistle *Cirsium arvense*	July – Sept.
daisy *Bellis perennis*	March – Oct.
daffodils *Narcissus* spp.	March – May
dames-violet (sweet rocket) *Hesperis*	
matronalis	May – July
dandelion *Taraxacum officinale*	March – July
dwarf thistle *Cirsium acaule*	July – Aug.
early-purple orchid *Orchis mascula*	April – May
field pansy *Viola arvensis*	April – Oct.
field scabious *Knautia arvensis*	May – Sept.
sweet-scented orchid *Gymnadenia*	
conopsea	June – Aug.
groundsel *Senecio vulgaris*	Feb. – Nov.
harebell *Campanula rotundifolia*	July – Sept.
hawkbits *Leontodon* spp.	June – Oct.
hawthorn *Crataegus monogyna*	May – June
hawthorn, two-styled or Midland	
C. laevigata	May – June
hazel *Corylus avellana*	March – April
heaths *Erica* spp.	Aug. – Sept.
hemp agrimony *Eupatorium cannabinum*	July – Sept.
honeysuckle *Lonicera periclymenum*	June – Sept.
hound's tongue *Cynoglossum officinale*	June – Aug.
ivy *Hedera helix*	Oct. – Nov.
kidney vetch *Anthyllis vulneraria*	June – Aug.
knapweeds *Centaurea* spp.	July – Sept.
lady's bedstraw *Galium verum*	July – Sept.
lady's smock *Cardamine pratensis*	April – June
lesser calamint *Calamintha nepeta*	July – Aug.
lesser bindweed *Convolvulus arvensis*	June – Aug.
less celandine *Ranunculus ficaria*	March – May
lime trees *Tilia* spp.	June – July
ling *Calluna vulgaris*	Aug. – Sept.
mallows *Malva/Lavatera/Althaea* spp.	June – Sept.
marjoram *Origanum vulgare*	July – Sept.
marsh woundwort *Stachys palustris*	July – Sept.
meadow saffron *Colchicum autumnale*	Sept. – Oct.
meadow vetchling *Lathyrus pratensis*	June – Sept.
monks-hood *Aconitum napellus*	May – June
moss campion *Silene acaulis*	July – Aug.
perennial or corn sow-thistle *Sonchus*	
arvensis	Aug. – Sept.
pinks *Dianthus* spp.	June – Sept.
potentillas (see cinquefoils)	
primrose *Primula vulgaris*	Feb. – May
purple-loosestrife *Lythrum salicaria*	June – Aug.
pyramidal orchid *Anacamptis pyramidalis*	June – Aug.
ragged-robin *Lychnis flos-cuculi*	May – June
ragworts *Senecio* spp.	May – Oct.
rape *Brassica napus*	May – Aug.
red bartsia *Odontites verna*	June – Aug.
red campion *Silene dioica*	May – June
red clover *Trifolium pratense*	May – Sept.
red valerian *Centranthus ruber*	June – Aug.
rock-roses *Helianthemum* spp.	May – Sept.
rose bay willowherb *Epilobium*	
angustifolium	July – Sept.
sea-holly *Eryngium maritimum*	July – Sept.
selfheal *Prunella vulgaris*	June – Sept.
soapwort *Saponaria officinalis*	Aug. – Oct.
sweet chestnut *Castanea sativa*	May
thrift *Armeria maritima*	March – Sept.
toadflaxes *Linaria* spp.	July – Oct.
water mint *Mentha aquatica*	Aug. – Sept.
white campion *Silene alba*	May – Sept.
white clover (dutch clover) *Trifolium*	
repens	May – Oct.
wild cherry *Prunus avium*	April – May
wild privet *Ligustrum vulgare*	June – July
wild thyme *Thymus drucei*	June – Aug.
willows (including sallows) *Salix* spp.	March – May
woundworts *Stachys* spp.	July – Sept.
yarrow *Achillea millefolium*	June – Aug.

Garden Flowers (Nomenclature: *RHS Dictionary of Gardening*, 1969)

ageratum *Ageratum* spp.	June – frost
alyssum *Alyssum maritimum*	May – Sept.
annual candytuft *Iberis umbellata*	June – Sept.
annual phlox *Phlox Drummondii*	July – Sept.
arabis *Arabis albida*	Feb. – June
astilbe *Astilbe* spp.	June – Aug.
aubrieta *Aubrieta deltoidea*	March – June
brambles, blackberries *Rubus* spp.	July – Sept.
butterfly bush *Buddleia davidii*	July – Oct.
button bush *Cephalanthus occidentalis*	Aug.
caryopteris *Caryopteris* × *Clandonensis*	Aug. – Sept.
catmint *Nepeta* × *Faassenii*	May – Sept.
ceanothus *Ceanothus dentatus*	May – June
clematis *Clematis* spp.	May – Oct.
coreopsis *Coreopsis* spp.	June – Sept.

cosmos *Cosmos bipinnatus*	Aug. – Sept.
dahlia *Dahlia*	July – frost
escallonia *Escallonia* spp.	June – Oct.
fleabane *Erigeron speciosus*	June – Aug.
geranium (pelargonium) *Pelargonium* vars.	May – Oct.
giant-leaved ragwort *Ligularia* (= *Senecio*) *clivorum*	July – Aug.
globe thistle *Echinops* spp.	July – Aug.
goldenrod *Solidago canadensis*	Aug. – Oct.
hawthorn, may *Crataegus laevigata* (*oxyacantha*)	May
heliotrope, cherry pie *Heliotropium peruvianum*	June – Oct.
honeysuckle *Lonicera* spp.	June – Oct.
hyssop *Hyssopus officinalis*	July – Sept.
'ice plant' *Sedum spectabile*	Sept. – Oct.
laurel *Prunus laurocerasus*	April
lavender *Lavandula* spp.	July – Sept.
lilacs *Syringa* spp.	May – June
marigolds, African & French *Tagetes* spp.	July – frost
Mexican orange *Choisya ternata*	April – May
Michaelmas daisy *Aster novi-belgii*; A. *foliaceus*	Sept. – Oct.
mignonette *Reseda odorata*	June – Oct.
night-scented stock *Matthiola bicornis*	July – Aug.
petunia *Petunia*	June – frost
primroses, polyanthus *Primula* spp.	March – May
privet *Ligustrum ovalifolium*	July
red-hot poker *Kniphofia* spp.	Aug. – Sept.
red valerian *Centranthus ruber*	June – Aug.
rock rose *Helianthemum nummularium*	June – July
rosemary *Rosmarinus officinalis*	May
Shasta daisy *Chrysanthemum maximum*	June – Aug.
shrubby veronicas *Hebe* spp.	May – Sept.
Siberian wallflower *Cheiranthus* × *Allionii*	May – July
sneezeweed *Helenium autumnale*	July – Sept.
sweet William *Dianthus barbatus*	June – July
tidy tips *Layia elegans*	June – Oct.
tobacco plant *Nicotiana* spp.	June – Sept.
vervain *Verbena* spp.	June – frost
viburnum *Viburnum* × *Burkwoodii*	March – May
Viburnum × *Carlcephalum*	April – May
viper's bugloss *Echium* spp.	June – Aug.
wallflower *Cheiranthus cheiri*	April – June
yellow alyssum, gold dust *Alyssum saxatile*	April – June
yellow knapweed *Centaurea macrocephala*	July

Appendix 5: Egg Sterilization

Materials
1 bottle of Milton (see note 4)
1 box of nappy liners
A shallow glass or plastic dish
A camel-hair paintbrush
Blotting paper

Method
Dilute 1 measure of Milton in 20 measures of water. Cut nappy liner into two

Remove 3–4 day-old eggs from host plant by cutting them from leaf with fine nail scissors or by using a camel-hair paintbrush moistened in diluted Milton

Place eggs in centre of piece of nappy liner and lower into dish containing diluted Milton until all eggs are covered. Any floating eggs can be pushed into fluid with the paintbrush.

Leave eggs immersed for 5 min., then raise edges of nappy liner to lift eggs out

Rinse thoroughly by running water over eggs in nappy liner. Take care not to let them float away.

Lay nappy liner on blotting paper or newspaper to absorb all water from underneath eggs. It is important to remove surplus moisture: a film of water left covering the eggs for an hour or more may kill the caterpillars inside

Place treated eggs in sterilized container to await emergence. Damp nappy liner will keep eggs from drying out and provide suitable surface for newly emerged larvae as their skins harden

Move newly hatched larvae to clean foodplant after 2 hr

Notes
1. A higher degree of sterilization can be achieved by transferring the eggs to the other half of the nappy liner and repeating the treatment using 10% formalin for 30 min. followed by washing and drying as previously directed. Care should be taken to ventilate the eggs thoroughly after the formalin sterilization and you *must not allow the Milton and formalin to mix during the treatment or even in the waste water*
2. Milton, if used undiluted, will quickly dissolve the egg shells, as will the diluted solution if the eggs are immersed for too long a time. Some species have tougher eggs than others and the effect of any accidental over-treatment can be observed with a good pocket lens or a microscope. The ribbing patterns on the surface of the egg will show signs of dissolving before there is serious damage so eggs should not be discarded unless they look severely damaged
3. Use undiluted Milton for wiping all working surfaces and to sterilize plastic and glass containers
4. Other propriety brands of bleach containing sodium hypochlorite can also be used for the procedures outlined above, but it is important to know the sodium hypochlorite content. Any brand used should be diluted to produce not more than 0.1% for egg sterilization and 2% to 5% for sterilizing cages and non-metallic containers

Appendix 6: Useful Addresses

Livestock
Entomological Livestock Supplies, Fairmile Road, Halesowen, West Midlands B63 3PZ
R.E. Stockley, 1 Marsh Street, Warminster, Wiltshire
The Living World, Seven Sisters Country Park, Exceat, Seaford, East Sussex
R.N. Baxter, 45 Chudleigh Crescent, Ilford, Essex IG3 9AT
Nature of the World, Fetcham Cottage, 19 Bell Lane, Fetcham, Leatherhead, Surrey
Brian Gardiner (cabbage whites for schools and laboratories), 18 Chesterton Hall Crescent, Cambridge
Worldwide Butterflies, Compton House, Sherborne, Dorset DT 4QN

Native Wild Flower and Grass Seedsmen
John Chambers, 15 Westleigh Road, Barton Seagrave, Kettering, Northants NN15 5AJ
  Has a variety of mixtures and provides information on management, quantity of seed required per hectare, etc. Separate list for bee and butterfly gardeners.
Emorsgate Seeds, Emorsgate, Terrington St Clement, King's Lynn, Norfolk PE34 4NY
  Wild-flower seed and various mixtures especially for landscaping, rather than for private gardens. Catalogue gives useful hints on care and management.
Suffolk Herbs (John Stevens), Sawyers Farm, Little Cornard, Sudbury, Suffolk
  Standard Mixtures, wild-flower seed and fifty-five species of herbs.

Flower Seedsmen
Suttons Seeds, Hele Road, Torquay, Devon TQ2 7QJ
Thompson & Morgan, London Road, Ipswich

Tropical-flower Seedsmen
Chiltern Seeds, Bortree Stile, Ulverston, Cumbria LA12 7PB
C.W. Hosking, Exotic Seed Importer, Camborne, Cornwall TR14 ONW

Specialist Plants and Shrubs
Hillier Nurseries (Winchester) Ltd., Ampfield House, Ampfield, Romsey, Hants SO5 9PA

Pollen
Messrs Sicapi, Boite Postale No. 5, 39330 Mouchard, Jura, France

Biological Controls
Natural Pest Control, 'Watermead', Yapton Road, Barnham, Bognor Regis, West Sussex PO22 OBQ

Entomological Equipment, Cages, etc
Messrs Watkins & Doncaster, Four Throws, Hawkhurst, Kent

Papronet
Direct Wire Ties Ltd, Wyke Works, Hedon Road, Hull, North Humberside

Greenhouse Heaters
W. Tombling Ltd, Telectric House, Winsover Road, Spalding, Lincs PE11 1EL
Findlay, Irvine Limited, Penicuik, Nr Edinburgh, Scotland

Professional Entomological Consultant
Claude Rivers, High Winds, 17 Cumnor Rise, Cumnor, Oxford

Greenhouse Magazine
Greenhouse, Haymarket Publications, 38/42 Hampton Road, Teddington, Middx TW11 OJE

Butterfly Houses
London Butterfly House, Syon Park, Brentford, Middlesex
Jersey Butterfly Farm, Haute Tombette, St Mary, Jersey, Channel Islands
Guernsey Butterfly Farm, Le Friquet, Castel, Guernsey, Channel Islands
New Forest Butterfly Farm, Longdown, Marchwood, Nr Southampton, Hampshire
The Butterfly Centre Eastbourne, Royal Parade, Eastbourne, Sussex
Worldwide Butterflies, Over Compton, Nr Yeovil, Somerset
Cotswold Wild Life Park Butterfly House, Burford, Gloucestershire

Societies for Butterfly and Wild Flower Conservation
Amateur Entomologists Society, Hon. General Secretary: S. A. A. Painter, 108 Hanover Avenue, Feltham, Middx TW13 4JP
Entomological Livestock Group, General Secretary: J. D. Steward, 14 Painswick Road, Cheltenham, Gloucestershire GL5 2HA
Exotic Entomology Group, B. Morris, 34 Borden Lane, Sittingbourne, Kent ME10 1DB
British Butterfly Conservation Society, Tudor House, Quorn, Loughborough, Leicestershire
Nature Conservancy Council, 19/20 Belgrave Square, London SW1
Botanical Society of the British Isles, Hon. General Secretary, c/o Dept. of Botany, British Museum (Natural History), Cromwell Road, London SW7 5BD
Royal Horticultural Society, Vincent Square, London SW1P 2PE
London Natural History Society, Secretary: Miss C.M. Balfour, 8 Crossfield Road, London NW3 4NS
Royal Society for Nature Conservation, The Green, Nettleham, Lincoln LN2 2NR

For Further Reading

British Butterflies

Brooks, Margaret M. and Charles Knight *A Complete Guide to British Butterflies* Cape 1982

Carter, David *Butterflies and Moths in Britain and Europe* Pan, London 1982

Emmel, Thomas C. *Butterflies: Their World* Thames & Hudson, London 1976

Ford, E.B. *Butterflies* (New Naturalist Series) Collins, London 1945

Health, J.H. (Ed.) *Provisional Atlas of the Insects of the British Isles* (Vol. I, Lepidoptera: Rhopalocra, Butterflies) Biological Record Centre, Huntingdon 1970

Higgins, L.G. & N.D. Riley *A Field Guide to the Butterflies of Britain and Europe* Collins, London, rev. edn 1980

Howarth, T.G. *South's British Butterflies* Warne, London 1973

Kettlewell, H.B.D. *Your Book of Butterflies and Moths* Faber & Faber, London 1963

Measures, David G. *Bright Wings of Summer* Prentice-Hall, Englewood Cliffe, N.J. 1976

Newman, L. Hugh with Moira Savonius *Create a Butterfly Garden* John Baker, London 1967

South, Richard *The Butterflies of the British Isles* Warne, London 1906 (and later editions)

South, Richard *The Moths of the British Isles* (2 vols) Warne, London 1907–08 (and later editions)

Whalley, Paul E.S. *Butterfly Watching* (Naturalist's Library) Severn House, London 1980

Other Butterflies

Brewer, Jo *Butterflies* Abrams, New York 1976

Common, I.S.B. and D.F. Waterhouse *Butterflies of Australia* Angus & Robertson, London & Sydney 1981

Corbet, A.S. and H.M. Pendlebury *The Butterflies of the Malay Penninsula* (revised: J.N. Eliot) Malay Nature Society, Kuala Lumpur, 3rd Edn 1978 (UK distrib: E.W. Classey, PO Box 93, Faringdon, Oxfordshire)

Johnston, Gweneth and Bernard *This is Hong Kong: Butterflies* Government Information Services, Hong Kong 1980

Laithwaite, Eric, Allan Watson and Paul E.S. Whalley *The Dictionary of Butterflies and Moths in Colour* Michael Joseph, London 1975

Owen, D.F. *Tropical Butterflies* Clarendon Press, Oxford 1971

Gardening, Wild and Cultivated Flowers

Bailey, L.H. *Manual of Cultivated Plants* Macmillan, New York

Beckett, Kenneth & Gillian *Planting Native Trees and Shrubs* Jarrold, Norwich 1979

Benson, Lyman *Plant Classification* Heath & Co., Lexington, Mass. and Toronto, 2nd edn 1979

Chittenden, F.J. (Ed.) *Dictionary of Gardening* (Vols 1–4 & Supplement) The Royal Horticultural Society, Clarendon Press, Oxford, 2nd edn 1956; 1969

Fitter, Richard & Alistair, & Marjorie Blamey *The Wild Flowers of Britain and Northern Europe* Collins, London 1974

Genders, Roy *Scented Flora of the World* Mayflower, London 1977

Hamilton, Geoff *The Gardeners' World Cottage Garden* BBC, London 1982

Hellyer, A.G.L. (ed.) *Sanders' Encyclopaedia of Gardening* Collingridge, London, 22nd edn 1952

Heywood, V.H. (Ed.) *Flowering Plants of the World* Oxford University Press, Oxford 1978

Johnson, Hugh *The Principles of Gardening* Mitchell Beazley, London 1979

McEwan, Helen *Seed Growers Guide to Herbs and Wild Flowers* Suffolk Herbs, Sudbury 1982

Martin, W. Keble *The New Concise British Flora* Michael Joseph and Ebury, London 1972 (new edition 1982)

Proctor, Michael & Peter Yeo *The Pollination of Flowers* (New Naturalist Series) Collins, London 1973

Ross-Craig, Stella *Drawings of British Plants* Pts I–XXXI, Bell, London 1948–73

Salisbury, Sir Edward *The Living Garden or the how and why of plant life* Bell & Sons, London, 2nd edn 1942

Salisbury, Sir Edward *Weeds and Aliens* (New Naturalist Series) Collins, London, 2nd edn 1964

Sanecki, Kay N. *The Fragrant Garden* Batsford, London 1981

Shepherd, F.W. *Hedges and Screens* (Wisley Handbook 17) Royal Horticultural Society, London 1974

Very, Rosemary *The Scented Garden* London 1981

Wells, Terry, Shirley Bell & Alan Frost *Creating Attractive Grasslands using Native Plant Species* Nature Conservancy Council 1981

Ecology

Hawksworth, D.L. (Ed.) *The Changing Flora and Fauna of Britain* Academic Press, London & New York 1974

Photography

Unno, Kazuo *Butterflies, their World* Kyoritsu Shuppan, Tokyo 1980

Conservation and the Law

Code of Conduct for the Conservation of Wild Plants Council for Environmental Conservation (CoEnCo) and the Botanical Society of the British Isles (BSBI), London 1982

Wild Life and the Law (No. 1: Wild Plants) CoEnCo & BSBI, London 1982

Weeds Act H.M.S.O. 1959

Wildlife and Countryside Act H.M.S.O. 1981

Index